Les Swan
503

On
Architecture

"Fred Rush's brilliant *On Architecture* is the most exciting thing I've read in the philosophy of art for years. It is full of fresh thinking and surprising – even daring – examples. He has rescued architecture from the formalists and the jargonists, and given it the place in philosophy that it enjoys in life. This is, to use Rush's term, 'deep aesthetics.'"

Arthur C. Danto, Columbia University

"As Fred Rush argues, various attempts over the last century to lend conceptual gravity to architecture have eclipsed our experience of it. *On Architecture*, his sustained and exacting reflection on the inevitably embodied nature of experience, returns to architecture the multi-sensory immersion foundational to its very perception. In adding material encounters to conceptual categories, Rush proposes not only that architecture is a distinct form of knowing, but that it also has the potential to enrich such elemental human faculties as memory and a sense of place."

Sandy Isenstadt, Yale University

Fred Rush is Associate Professor of Philosophy at the University of Notre Dame. He is the editor of the *Cambridge Companion to Critical Theory* (2004).

Praise for the series

'. . . allows a space for distinguished thinkers to write about their passions.'

The Philosophers' Magazine

'. . . deserve high praise.'

Boyd Tonkin, *The Independent* (UK)

'This is clearly an important series. I look forward to reading future volumes.'

Frank Kermode, author of *Shakespeare's Language*

'. . . both rigorous and accessible.'

Humanist News

'. . . the series looks superb.'

Quentin Skinner

'. . . an excellent and beautiful series.'

Ben Rogers, author of *A.J. Ayer: A Life*

'Routledge's Thinking in Action series is the theory junkie's answer to the eminently pocketable Penguin 60s series.'

Mute Magazine (UK)

'Routledge's new series, Thinking in Action, brings philosophers to our aid . . .'

The Evening Standard (UK)

'. . . a welcome new series by Routledge.'

Bulletin of Science, Technology and Society (Can)

'Routledge's innovative new Thinking in Action series takes the concept of philosophy a step further'

The Bookwatch

FRED RUSH

On
Architecture

Routledge
Taylor & Francis Group

NEW YORK AND LONDON

First edition published 2009
by Routledge
270 Madison Ave, New York, NY 10016

Simultaneously published in the UK
by Routledge
2 Park Square, Milton Park, Abingdon, Oxon OX14 4RN

Routledge is an imprint of the Taylor & Francis Group, an informa business

© 2009 Taylor & Francis

Typeset in Joanna MT and DIN by
RefineCatch Limited, Bungay, Suffolk
Printed and bound in the United States of America on acid-free paper by
Edwards Brothers, Inc.

All rights reserved. No part of this book may be reprinted or
reproduced or utilized in any form or by any electronic,
mechanical or other means, now known or hereafter
invented, including photocopying and recording, or in any
information storage or retrieval system, without permission in
writing from the publishers.

Trademark Notice: Product or corporate names may be trademarks or registered
trademarks, and are used only for identification and explanation without intent
to infringe.

Library of Congress Cataloging-in-Publication Data
Rush, Fred Leland.
   On architecture / Fred Rush.—1st ed.
      p. cm.—(Thinking in action)
   Includes bibliographical references and index.
   1. Architecture–Human factors.   2. Architecture–Philosophy.   I. Title.
   NA2542.4.R87 2008
   720.1—dc22   2008021338

ISBN10: 0–415–39618–2 (hbk)
ISBN10: 0–415–39619–0 (pbk)

ISBN13: 978–0–415–39618–9 (hbk)
ISBN13: 978–0–415–39619–6 (pbk)

List of Figures

Preface

The series for which this book is written, Thinking in Action, stresses accessibility for the non-expert to issues that have pending importance in the subject matters addressed by its books. I have taken this brief very seriously and, as a consequence, fear that philosophers, philosophy professors, architects, and architecture professors will not be impressed with the depth of treatment. Of course I hope this is not true, but one has to be realistic. Nevertheless, I do think the issues the book addresses are timely and will consider the time writing it well spent if it is a catalyst to further thought on the topics it treats.

I have chosen three topics: the role of phenomenology in architectural theory and practice, the relation of architecture to other arts, and the role of architecture in urban and suburban design. There are a host of other concerns that one might treat in a book like this, but I see these as three very important issues, and I have chosen to address them and order them in the book as I have so that I can tie them together in a particular way. Although there are historical, social, and political issues that would have to be addressed more fully in any omnibus treatment of the significance of architecture, I emphasize the role of perceptual experience.[1] Some architects seem to take for granted how their products are experienced or, more charitably, think of the experience of them as having ancillary importance. Modern architectural practice has tended to be a hermetic art, at least when viewed from outside the profession. Modern architectural theory can be similarly insular. Style, semiotic meaning, and the historical referentiality of buildings to other buildings are just some of the intra-disciplinary concerns that exert a strong influence within the discipline. The meaning of buildings becomes a question of what they represent, express, or exemplify.[2] Human beings and their experiential capacities can tend to drop out of the picture when these kinds of concerns predominate. Of course, these matters can touch upon experience, but they tend to do so superficially, involving, typically, claims concerning the look of a structure or its function. Even when architects do build with experience in mind, they often "under-theorize" the terms in which buildings are experienced.

Under-theorization is not always a defect of course. One doesn't need to have a theory of everything or in every domain. It might be fine not to have one of the human experience of architecture if the architecture that were built happened to answer to the claims of human experience as a matter of course or if, for some reason, humans didn't happen to demand a theory in this locale. But neither of these conditions is met, at least not in the modern world. If there is anything modern people want to understand more than experience, I want to know what that is. And modern architects are chief purveyors of theories of what they do and why. So, having a basically adequate account of what sort of experience architecture aims at is not, for the modern world at least, optional. Some architects, as it turns out, do have very interesting ideas in this regard, but these ideas tend to be difficult to pin down. That's not exactly the fault of the architects—they are, after all, artists, and very few artists are adept at clearly stating in a theoretical way what they do and why. One might even say that they can't be adept at this, or at least can't be without theory becoming an obstacle to their creation. Part of what I hope to do in this book is to speak in a non-technical way (both philosophically and architecturally) about one approach to architectural experience that I believe holds promise, and to discuss it in relation to some concrete examples. This approach is one I call "phenomenological" but, as anyone with a passing familiarity with twentieth-century European philosophy and art criticism will tell you, that term can mean many things, so I will have to qualify it. This phenomenological approach to architecture is the primary subject matter of the first chapter, but it also informs my treatment of the relation of architecture to other arts in Chapter 2 and the role of architecture in urban and suburban planning in Chapter 3. Although the book is titled On Architecture, in order to capture its basic phenomenological bent, it might just as well have been called On Architectural Space.

One of my claims is, more precisely, that phenomenological analyses of being embodied are central to understanding large swaths of the experience of architecture. This saddles me with a problem. There are photographs of architecture in the book but, for reasons of cost, they are few and in black and white. In itself that is bad enough, but it is not the main problem. It is particularly discouraging in a book on the phenomenology of architecture that stresses bodily experience that there is not a dynamic way to convey what it is like to move through the spaces that it discusses. Photographs cannot hope to do that, and they even mislead. That is one reason why architects are so choosy about the photographers they authorize to portray their buildings. The only way to have given even partly a sense of moving through a building would have been to have included a CD-ROM "virtual tour" with the book. Again, the cost would be prohibitive. Some websites for famous buildings provide such tours: they tend to be rudimentary but are still better than photographs. Yet even this is not like being in a building and, it might be argued, there is even more chance of being misled than with photographs, since the "movement" in a CD-ROM might dupe one into thinking of that movement as a suitable replacement for the first-hand experience of moving through the actual building. No one would make that mistake, ones hopes, if a photograph were in question.

Even though I discuss some buildings at fair length, in a book of this brevity it is not easy to focus in-depth on single examples. I can't hope to discuss the construction and materiality of works with as much specificity or authority as, say, a Michael Caldwell or an Edward Ford. That notwithstanding, the building I have chosen for the most extended treatment, Steven Holl's Nelson-Atkins Museum extension, is architecture built with phenomenology in mind and is, for the present, one of the supreme examples of this approach to building. Consideration of this example provides a way to put phenomenological thinking about architecture into action, as the title of this series of books mandates.

One last caveat: this is a book primarily about modern architecture and planning. That fact does not conceal a judgment on my part that modern architecture is an evolutionary terminus for architecture generally or that modernist architecture is otherwise superior to other sorts. It reflects two things. First, although all architecture has its phenomenology, building with phenomenology explicitly in mind is a modern practice. That's just historical fact. Although one could argue, I suppose, that there might have been proto-phenomenological thought in architecture in earlier periods, a pretty Pickwickian sense of "phenomenology" would be abroad in such an argument. The second thing the restriction of the book to modern architecture reflects is that modern architecture constitutes the architectural present tense. It is where we are, architecturally speaking. Now, there are claims that one should carefully distinguish modern architecture as a purely temporal period of architectural activity from architectural modernism, that is, architecture practiced according to certain normative principles that govern what it means to be modern. But I have used and will use the terms "modern" and "modernist" interchangeably. Although there are all sorts of buildings being built in modern times, I am just Hegelian enough to think that modernist architecture is at the core of the modern period and, therefore, is the context in which the discussion of the relation of architecture to phenomenology best takes place.

Acknowledgments

I am grateful to Dana Knapp and Laura Kline of the Nelson-Atkins Museum for their aid during my visits there and for access to the architectural archive for the Bloch Addition to the museum. Years ago as a graduate student in philosophy I was fortunate to be able to moonlight in the architectural studio of Gins + Arakawa and to be involved in the preparation of a retrospective of their work at the Guggenheim Museum. Many of the ideas here were developed in *nuce* then in conversation with Madeline Gins and Arakawa. I am indebted to Dennis Doordan, Gregg Horowitz, and Stephen Watson for written comments on a draft of the manuscript. Thanks also to Tony Bruce, Kate Ahl, and Michael Andrews of Routledge, and Katy Carter of Swales & Willis, who made editing the book a pleasure.

My wife Leslie and our sons Nicholas and Matthew selflessly allowed me the time away from family commitments to complete this book. My love to them for that and much else.

Parts of Chapter 1 were presented as a paper, "L'Architecture procédurale et profounde," at the Université Paris IX in spring 2006.

Notes on References

Too many endnotes are always a distraction and no more so than in a book like this, which is not addressed primarily to academic architectural theorists or professional philosophers. I have tried to keep the notes few in number and terse in content. I have indulged myself a bit in Chapter 2, where I include four rather long and involved notes devoted to the exposition of German Idealism's systematic treatment of architecture. These notes are meant for those who might be interested in a bit more information on this topic than the text itself provides, but can be skipped by those who aren't interested in the subject matter they cover. I have marked each of these notes with an asterisk so that skipping them is facilitated.

I refer to Merleau-Ponty's work fairly often in Chapter 1 and have made those references parenthetically in the text. I employ standard English translations where they are available. I note any changes in translation by me.

The abbreviations of works of Merleau-Ponty are:

PP   *The Phenomenology of Perception*, C. Smith trans., 6th edn. (London & New York: Routledge, 1974). Original: *Phénoménologie de la perception* (Paris: Gallimard, 1945).

SB   *The Structure of Behaviour*, A.L. Fisher trans. (Boston: Beacon, 1963). Original: *La structure du comportement* Paris: (PUF, 1942).

VI   *The Visible and the Invisible*, A. Lingis trans. (Evanston: Northwestern University Press, 1968). Original: *Le visibile et l'invisibile* (Paris: Gallimard, 1964).

One

Humans began to build the structures that have come through history to be considered architecture because they required shelter. These structures, as best we know, began by improving upon given natural formations that could provide shelter: a typical example would be a cave, minimally adapted. In some environments, of course, there are no suitable natural structures and so building for shelter developed. Building for shelter is a very important skill and so, over time, the craft of building developed and was handed down from generation to generation. It is unclear exactly when the skill became something along the lines of an expertise, to which some sort of division of labor would be appropriate. Because shelter is one of the most basic ways to remake the world in terms that make it hospitable to humans, it is easy to see why buildings came to play important religious and cultural roles beyond mere physical protection and why the skill of building might be prized as an art. A basic feature of early religion, anthropologists agree, is the attempt to understand and temper a nature that is radically beyond human control by calling its blessings down to the tribe through ritual. This magical thought presupposes understanding nature as having will or as the product of a will. Although it is perhaps not strictly necessary to conceive of nature as an entity that is willed in order to conceive of it as something that will answer to one's supplications, viewing nature anthropomorphically is a predominating way to make these ideas cohere. If one views making shelter as taking something away from nature (by remaking it) in order to protect oneself against it, one might very well give thanks or seek forgiveness for the material or the violation, necessary though it might be. This train of thought seems nowadays quite antiquated, but the idea that a base meaning of architecture involves a place of dwelling, one that focuses divine attributes and thereby roots one to place, still interests philosophers and religious thinkers. For them the concept of dwelling is of central importance, not just for explicating the historical beginnings of architecture but in thinking about the present-day ethical significance of buildings.[1]

There may be good arguments why architecture should be seen mainly as still involved with these issues of dwelling. Perhaps our mechanistic and informational age has led us to "forget," as Heidegger might say, important truths about architecture of this sort. No one, presumably, will deny the common sense idea that architecture can or should lie at the heart of social community and self-understanding that is part and parcel of this idea of dwelling. But much of the thought on dwelling as a basic concept with which to approach architecture is strongly metaphysical, subject to long and tortuous argument and historical analysis and, to some, seems unacceptably atavistic, perhaps even committing a rather grand and convoluted instance of the genetic fallacy. I will not be discussing this strand of twentieth-century thought on architecture, not because I think it is wrong, but because much of what it aims at securing for architecture in terms of cultural significance can be ensured by a different approach. I am concerned to redirect the consideration of the significance of architecture along lines that have to do with the concept of being embodied.

Approaching questions of the meaning of architecture through an investigation of the nature of human embodied experience has two main rationales. The first has to do with considering architecture in terms of *experience*. There are few, if any, artifacts crafted by humans that afford the enveloping complexity of a building. Phenomenology generally is most useful in assessing the nature of perception or other forms of consciousness that fall short of explicit conception. These are aspects of experience whose structure and richness are over-looked by theories that are fine-tuned to account for "higher-order" cognition. For purposes of illustration, by limiting ourselves to perceptual awareness it becomes immediately obvious how complex, deep, and all-inclusive the experience of architecture can be. To borrow a commonplace idea from home audio and theater, architecture is the ultimate surround-sound experience translated in more directly spatial terms. One is surrounded by a building: at any turn of the head, or any other bodily part, one is presented with new visual, auditory, and tactile experience; and these experiences are, in virtue of the fact that no one occupies a completely stable, immobile perspective from moment to moment of perception, constantly changing in novel ways. Moreover, conscious perception is influenced, as we shall discuss more fully later in this chapter, by more implicit and perhaps in some sense un- or pre-conscious states having to do with motion and bodily equilibrium that are also responsive to being ensconced in architectural space.

Now, one might say, landscape can also surround one in this way. This is certainly true and one need not deny this in order to see how unique architecture is in this experiential regard. For architecture, unlike a canyon or prairie, is *made* to elicit such response and that fact "loops back" on one's experience of it. And, to pick up on the second part of the formulation above, the experience of architecture, perhaps especially of it, is bound up with the experience of one's body as the medium for that experience. For this reason, an adequate experiential account of architecture must include an analysis of embodied experience. Indeed, if one wished to compound matters and were not afraid of being a little coy, one might interpret the claim that embodied experience is an important component of an overall treatment of the significance of architecture in a bifurcated way: the experience is embodied in that it is experience had by means of the body as the seat of perception, *and* it is also embodied because the architecture itself, as a complex body, impels experience in that way.

Ignoring this aspect of architectural experience can lead to an impoverished and false account of that experience. I'll mention two potential problems briefly here, and wait until later in this chapter to address the problems more comprehensively. Perhaps the worst outcome of ignoring the embodied nature of architectural experience is that the very idea of experience can drop out of consideration. This does not happen often. But what has happened, especially in the literature by architects and architectural theorists at the beginning and end of the twentieth century (the mid-century is better in this regard), is that the idea of experience takes such a back seat to other ways of understanding architecture that it all but disappears. There are many forms of this disappearance but the emphasis on the historical inter-textuality of buildings (i.e., the idea that buildings are to be understood

first and foremost in terms of their position in the history of
architecture) and semiological approaches to architecture,
whether structuralist or deconstructive, tend to push phenomenologically inspired analyses that stress experience to
the side. One might call this the "buildings about buildings"
movement. Proponents of such historicist and semiological
approaches may think that is all to the good. Perhaps phenomenology as a methodology is of only local historical
interest and has been superseded by the other approaches.
Most of these claims either have an abecedarian take on what
phenomenology is, that tends to stall it in the horse latitudes
of an early point in the history of the phenomenological
movement when philosophers embraced "pure" phenomenology and reject it as utopian formalism, or they fail to realize
how much certain strands of the phenomenological approach
live on in work that they consider canonical (e.g., Foucault,
Derrida, Gadamer, etc.) For these reasons and others, I am
skeptical of claims that phenomenology is a has-been enter-
prise. Second, there is an untoward result of inadequate attention to the embodied experience of architecture that obtains
within the concept of experience. This is a simplified and falsi-
fying reduction of what range of experience is pertinent to
architecture to the visual and, indeed, to a particular view of
what counts under the heading of "the visual." Humans can and
often rightly do think abstractly in terms of geometric form,
pattern, or design outside of purely mathematical contexts.
But one aspect of this sort of experience is a felt remoteness
from one's own body. Aesthetic theories—and architectural
theories among them—have developed in modern times in
terms that give vision, and this particular abstract understanding of vision, pride of place. Understanding a piece of architecture in these terms—in terms of its look—is really but one

aspect of the significance of architecture, even if one thinks of architectural rather formally. And, if one just substitutes this aspect of experience of architecture for the whole of it, one will get a wildly skewed idea of that significance, no more or less so than if I replaced the experience of music with the experience of Baroque counterpoint or the experience of playing football with that of taking penalty kicks.

To put the point bluntly, then, architecture is part of what some social scientists call "material culture," and understanding it, its history, and its potential requires an approach that does justice to this fact. Moreover, understanding architecture as material culture must encompass what I take to be a brute fact, i.e., that architecture is a way for humans to reflect on what it is to be the kind of embodied forms of intelligence they are. This reflection, in turn, is material, i.e., it involves material engagements with buildings, with those that are products of explicit, theoretically driven architectural activity and with those that are not (what archimanes sometimes contrast as architect vs. non-architect buildings). Phenomenology that is open to a description and analysis of human material engagement is a promising point of entry into some forms of basic architectural significance that might otherwise go unexamined.

TWO WAYS OF SEEING THINGS

The philosopher who has given the most systematic thought to being embodied is the French phenomenologist Maurice Merleau-Ponty (1908–1961).[2] Merleau-Ponty was concerned to describe and explicate a phenomenon that he considered basic to human experience—what it is like to be an embodied consciousness. Others before him had raised this question, sometimes from similar perspectives, e.g., the

German phenomenologist and philosopher of mathematics Edmund Husserl and Husserl's student Martin Heidegger—but it is Merleau-Ponty who develops his thought on the matter farthest. Merleau-Ponty died relatively young while still working out his formulation of both the question "what is it like to be embodied?" and its answer. Some have argued that his best insights on the question and answer can be found in his unfinished work and even that the later work signals a fundamental reformulation of both the question and its answer. The main text cited on behalf of this interpretation is *The Visible and the Invisible* (1964). Gary Gutting has argued persuasively that one should be wary of reading too much into this text; I shall try to heed that warning in what follows and do justice to the fact that *The Phenomenology of Perception* (1945) is Merleau-Ponty's main statement of his views.[3] Nevertheless, I shall focus on some of the terminology deployed in Merleau-Ponty's later work, if for no other reason than that phenomenologically oriented architects have embraced it.

Merleau-Ponty develops his account of being embodied by contrasting it with two other ways that one might think of the relation of minds to the world that figure prominently in the history of philosophy and in the empirical sciences of the modern period. (By this I mean what historians of philosophy call "modern," dating roughly from the writings of Descartes in the first half of the seventeenth century up to those of Immanuel Kant in the latter half of the eighteenth.) One needn't follow Merleau-Ponty's precise analysis of the competing camps in the mind/body wars in order to find his own manner of solving the dispute interesting in itself and for architecture. But since, in his own case, his alternative to the competing approaches follows upon this analysis, it pays to rehearse it.

The first traditional way to think of the relation of mind to world in the modern period is what Merleau-Ponty calls "empiricism" or, alternatively, either "realism" or "objectivism." Empiricism begins with the world and understands the mind in terms of it. For instance, the relations of association between mental items, e.g., ideas, beliefs, etc., are construed in physical terms as causal and law-like. Some in the empiricist camp take this thought quite far and argue that mental causation is just a form of physical causation— what some contemporary philosophers call "reductivism"— but one needn't make such an argument to count as an "empiricist" in the sense that Merleau-Ponty uses the word. The other way to understand the mind to world relation is to stress, instead, the mental side of the relation. This Merleau-Ponty calls "intellectualism" or "idealism." An intellectualist accounts for the structure of the non-mental world in terms given by the structure of the mental. There are, as with empiricism, many versions of this idea. Some intellectualists favor the view that the basic cognitive features according to which the world is structured are implanted in the mind either divinely (e.g., Descartes, and the philosopher and mathematician Gottfried Leibniz) or naturally (e.g., the linguist Noam Chomsky). Others opt for an account of the power of the mental over the structure of the non-mental that construes the former as a necessary theoretical condition on the very possibility of the other. This view was made famous by Kant and can be found in some of the German Idealists who came directly after Kant and took themselves to be elaborating this thought. On this truly idealist view, the world "as it is"—i.e., as it is when one subtracts out the idea of all mental structuring from it—is indifferentiable. It might have structure of its own, but no one (except perhaps God) could know it as so structured. Inversely, any consciousness is determinate, at least to a degree—the notion of diffuse awarenesses is anathema to the idealist (PP 28–9). Consciousness, as a synthetic mental activity, is what constructs objects out of nothing but particulate chaos (PP 29).

It is important to see that the two rival ways to see things share both a presumption and a problem (PP 39–41). The shared presumption is that mind and world are radically different things. The problem—and it is a problem that persists into the present for adherents of these creeds—is that, once so separated, it is quite challenging to get mind and world back together. A picture of things that posits minds on the one side and the world on the other without an account of how the two modes of things coexist and interact contradicts both experience and observation. But getting a third thing into position to broker the interaction is extremely difficult. In the history of philosophy there is a marked tendency to conceive of the third thing more along one line or the other (i.e., as mostly pertaining to mind or, alternatively, to world) and, thus, risk it being not a third thing at all. There are lots of these sorts of problems—problems of dualism—at many levels of analysis. But it is not necessary to enumerate them here; it is enough to see that this problem is one that a philosopher would be very strongly motivated to avoid. It is also important to see that the human body places that problem front and center. There are all sorts of things that we know about human bodies by observing and theorizing about them as physical objects. Medical science depends upon this approach to the nature of human bodies. But being "in" a human body is not like a volume of liquid being in a bottle— the preposition "in" does not work here to denote spatial containment. Our relation to our bodies, physical though they are, is much more intimate than that, and such intimacy was ordinarily thought to be the mark of the mental. "What could be more intimate to me than my thoughts?" was the idea.

Merleau-Ponty claims that the shared premise and problem just discussed go hand in glove. Indeed, he thinks that once one introduces a divide between mind and world one must have the problem of dualism and that the problem is insuperable. He doesn't actually *prove* that it is insuperable but appeals to experience to claim that nowhere in it is there a need to posit the basic constituents that empiricism and intellectualism do. Merleau-Ponty disputes the shared premise and, in so doing, hopes to steer clear of the dualistic problems. Phenomenology, the methodology that Merleau-Ponty advocated and practiced, obliges one to begin by describing how things appear without any antecedent pre-interpretation of the data. At its most general, this admonition and injunction to "merely describe" means neither to affirm nor to deny any claim having to do with the purported objective status of things. Roughly, this is what phenomenologists mean when they demand a "suspension of judgment" as the starting point of analysis.[4] What is important is that the methodology gives Merleau-Ponty a way around the empiricist/intellectualist impasse. Both traditions diverge from the way things are: if one does not prejudice one's view of the phenomena by antecedently bringing to bear categories like "mind," "physical," "body," "cause," etc. this result can be avoided. Minds and bodies do interact and they do so all the time. They do not appear to be participants in radically different orders of things, at least not when it comes to the *experience* of them. For Merleau-Ponty, that is, the mind and world are not fundamentally separate. The challenge he faces is articulating their

point of connection with the philosophical vocabulary at his
disposal—a vocabulary tooled in the lathe of history in order
to discuss the problem in precisely the dualist terms he
ultimately wants to reject.

A THIRD WAY

Merleau-Ponty begins with mind and world in an indissol-
uble bond. The human point of contact with this bond is the
body, and Merleau-Ponty shifts his vocabulary for talking
about consciousness in terms of it. The central claim of
The Phenomenology of Perception is that the body is what per-
ceives. Care has to be taken to understand this correctly. By
"body" Merleau-Ponty does not mean the physical body as it
would be observed and measured by the standards of modern
physics or chemistry. That idea of body certainly has its
place, as we have said, but that place is local and contextual.
The relevant locality is the empirical sciences: their theories
and aims give that sense of body its contextual meaning. By
"body" Merleau-Ponty means a conscious and potentially
self-conscious body, for which the world is not something
else that is given to it for extra-worldly processing but is,
rather, what the body is already embedded in. What we find
when we look at the experience of our bodies is that they
cannot be objects for us in the first instance. Scientific study
requires one to objectify the body, i.e., consider it apart from
at least many of the modes of experience that belong to it. The
fact that one can do this does not, however, mean that in
attaining this remoteness from the body one is discovering its
utmost nature. Experiencing one's own body primarily or
only as an object is possible: there are pathologies in which
the experience of body is so objectified—forms of psychosis,
radical dissociation, and, perhaps, certain epistemological or

social deformations like false consciousness or extreme ideological thought, although that is contestable. But these modes of experience are exceptional.

We have an intimate, pre-objective awareness and understanding of our bodies. Perception being "pre-objective" means that, at that level of awareness, there is no experiential distinction between "subject" and "object," at least as those terms are characteristically deployed in the theory of knowledge, metaphysics, the philosophy of psychology, and the empirical sciences. That, in turn, means that the character of such experience is indeterminate—one can only contrast and discriminate one thing over and against another if the basic contrast between "I" and "it" is available. In the perception of one's body there is no logical space, so to speak, between the consciousness and body; body and the awareness of body are co-mingled and, to that extent, are unified. Merleau-Ponty is so concerned that the idea of consciousness as it has developed in Western philosophy is so bound up with the idea of being separate from its focus—our bodies and other objects—that he sometimes writes that one should abandon the idea of consciousness altogether.

Merleau-Ponty and many of his readers have tried to express the relation of mind to world according to this "third way" in a number of fashions. In my view these are often hamstrung by Merleau-Ponty's own continued fealty to the language of dualism (usually of an intellectualist sort). As a result, the concepts that he deploys to depict the place of mind in the world can leave the connection of mind and world just as occult as mind–world dualism makes the point of connection out to be. In fact, Merleau-Ponty came to see this as a deficit in his own thought and, at the time of his death, seemed to be altering his mode of expression to rid his thought of residual intellectualism. I shall talk a bit about Merleau-Ponty's terminology below, but it is helpful at first to sweep the floor of the history of concepts used to solve the problem of mind–world interaction and start over. In doing so, I shall try to set out the better, less intellectualist, version of Merleau-Ponty's theory. I believe this view to be latent in The Phenomenology of Perception, although imperfectly expressed there.

A central insight of Merleau-Ponty's "third way" is that the relation of mind to world is best thought of as between part and whole and not as one involving the unity of two fundamentally disparate existential regions, one of which transcends or exists outside of the other. Think of the world as a whole as a structured system and mind as a part of that system. As a part, mind has its native structure as well, and that structure is what it is by virtue of being part of the overall system of the world. Even though mind is a proper part of the system of the world as a whole, there are also structures of the world that are not mind-like. Now, some of the structural properties of mind are that it is conscious, can be self-conscious, can be theoretical, etc. Call this the "reflective" structure of mind. Moreover, because mind has such reflective properties it is able, at least at reasonably explicit and articulate levels of reflection, to take the world and mind's place in it as an object on which it may reflect. Perhaps this is even a necessary or essential property of having a mind or, more narrowly, having a human mind.

So far, so good. But there are two complications. The first is that it seems that being able to take the world and mind's place in it as an object for reflection introduces the danger of seeing the mind not just as a part of the overall structure of the world, but as detachable from that structure in some way.

This introduces an impulse for transcendence that lands one in the dualism we have just discussed (and many others, as well). Why? Here one must speculate. Perhaps, as Nietzsche thought, the impulse is part of a defense mechanism that is put in motion in order to deflect from awareness, or even compensate for, the many ways in which humans are vulnerable (we aren't good sight hunters, we don't run as fast as a gazelle, we don't breed quickly, etc.). Or perhaps, as Spinoza believed, it is just a structural property of this particular finite bit of the infinite whole of all things: we can "emend the intellect" to try to overcome it but it is still more or less hardwired. A second complication is that, even though mind is a part of the overall world structure, contained entirely "within" that world, it is not a hermetically sealed part of it. "Having a mind," "being a mind," "mindedness"—however one wants to refer to the sub-part—exists on a continuum that extends well into areas that seem to blur the boundary of the part and other parts of the whole of the world, especially from the perspective of the mind. This is why I qualified a bit above and did not just identify "being minded" with "being conscious." Philosophers often have considered consciousness—understood minimally as directed mental focus—to be the basic state of mindedness in humans. The concept has also often been used as a way to draw lines between human mentality and animal "behavior." Merleau-Ponty vigorously challenges drawing this line as is commonly done in philosophy. "Mindedness" will also include many states or processes that may seem "unfocused" or "merely behavioral" if viewed from the perspective of theories of mind that adopt directed consciousness as a benchmark for mind. There is no bright line that separates consciousness from behavior on this view; they bleed into one another as the structural properties that typify the mind part of the whole of the world blend in with other structures of the world that are not mental.

My attempt at simplifying Merleau-Ponty may still seem pretty abstract, but it does have the merit of being less metaphorical than Merleau-Ponty's own writing on these matters. To be fair, he is attempting—as would any phenomenologist worth his salt—to describe the experience of one who is a subpart of the whole, and that means taking on board in that description the impacts on experience of (a) being somewhat misled about the nature of the part of which one is a member and (b) the dawning realization that one has been so misled. Perhaps Merleau-Ponty puts things as he does in order to capture those complications experientially. As I mentioned before, Merleau-Ponty prefers to drop the term "consciousness" when he talks about human beings' basic ways of orienting themselves in the world. Because he stresses that being human is not something outside of the world, he also hesitates to use the preposition "in" when talking about the place of mind. Much more common in his writings are statements that mind is "within," "among," or "alongside" other parts of the world. Merleau-Ponty's hesitancy to draw absolute lines between "higher order" cognition and subpersonal or affective experience is shown by the terms he can tend to use to talk most generally about how one is in the world by being minded, e.g., "comportment" (*comportement*), a French adaptation of a technical term from Heidegger's German, *Verhalten*. In everyday French and German both terms can mean "behavior," but what Heidegger and Merleau-Ponty mean by the term is decidedly not brute, consciousness-opaque, merely dispositional physical movement—i.e., what behaviorists like B.F. Skinner and W.V.O. Quine would call behavior—it is rather what the philosopher Hubert Dreyfus nicely glosses as "orientation," which includes cognitive, emotive, mood-like and skilled structures of "coping."[5]

To recapitulate: Merleau-Ponty holds that the body is the point at which the mind and the other parts of the world overlap. The contrast between figure and ground (or between foreground and background) is how Merleau-Ponty explicates the basic structure or schema of what he calls the "lived body" (PP 51ff., 60). As I mentioned in my mock-up of Merleau-Ponty's account of phenomenology and of the relation between mind and body, this distinction is not the product of judgment or of any other cognitive act in which parts are related through a mental synthesis or other combination. The contrast is key to a variety of non-conceptual forms of awareness, including basic somatic states of being oriented in the world—for instance, touch. When Merleau-Ponty speaks of "perception" he means to include just this sort of basic, pre-conscious understanding. Now, calling these orientations "understanding" can seem odd because some philosophers reserve the term for mental states that have "content," that is, states that have determinate meaning for one. If one assumes that "meaning" is a concept properly limited to discriminating, reflective awareness—say, judgment—then one will not include what Merleau-Ponty counts as perception among meaningful states. But Merleau-Ponty's point is precisely that the reflective states are only meaningful because they have components that are already meaningful in their own right. He thinks that it is simply a prejudice to insist on restricting meaning to what is accessible to and articulated by reflection. There are many ways that we understand the world implicitly, and it is only on the basis of those understandings that anything like theoretical understanding is possible, not the other way around. That is of course not to say that those understandings are always correct or ·that reflective understanding is second best. But it is to insist that implicit, pre-conceptual understanding is genetically primary.

Merleau-Ponty was well-versed in the experimental psychology of his day and presents a number of very detailed case histories in the literature to support his views. The most famous of these is the case of "Schneider" (PP 103ff.).[6] Schneider has suffered an injury that has left him unable correctly to produce behavior in response to abstract commands unless he first observes the pertinent parts of his body. When prompted he cannot describe when his arms are at rest next to his body and cannot tell where on his body he is being touched without matching the experience to one in which he touches himself on that spot. He cannot point to his nose but can grasp it. Schneider's bodily experience of external objects is similarly impoverished. For example, he cannot visualize objects on command that are not present to him. Still, he can hold objects, e.g., place his hand on his body or light a cigarette. The main point of the examples is that Schneider can function perfectly well when in practical environments that he is used to. He has no problem performing the tasks of his factory work, for instance. It is when the issue of representing those functions to himself is introduced into the experimental context that there are problems. Such representation is not required for many actions and any theory of action that treats representation as necessary in this regard is false. Merleau-Ponty argues that neither empiricism nor intellectualism can account for Schneider's syndrome because they both require representation to play an essential role in the explanation of action. Empiricism would characteristically require one to be able to represent a body part in order to move it and would look for a physical breakdown that short-circuits a causal connection between the sensory modality responsible for the representation of observation and behavior. It seems that what is absent in Schneider's case is the constant conjunction of space and touch in a unified, embodied form of experience, not experience that is triggered by observation. The intellectualist can do no better. Schneider cannot conceptualize the world spatially. Take the example of pointing at his nose. That is a response that requires more than mere habitual action. It presupposes knowing what "pointing" means, while grasping only requires a disposition to respond differentially to stimuli. The intellectualist would require an interposing conception or inference for action to occur, yet this is not necessary.

Merleau-Ponty's own way of handling Schnieder cases should be apparent. What has happened to Schneider is that a part of a whole integrated system of embodied consciousness has failed. What remains is a sub-system of pre-objective orientations that are spatial, but do not operate with the concept "space," as would be required were objective space at issue. Nor is "grasping his nose" merely physical: it is meaningful, although not reflectively so (at least not for Schneider). Mind and body are not two separate systems that belong together as an aggregate; one subtends the other.

Let's pause and take stock once more. My body is (a) ever-present to me, (b) not primordially an object for me, and (c) something that I move with, not something I move, i.e., it has the characteristic of direct motility—I do not have to place my body in order to move. But (d) my body is also a unity. I can move my hand but not just my hand. The movement is part of a whole coordinated way that the lived body is for me at that time. Spatiality—the experience of space both of the body and of other things—is, then, an extension of the lived body. The proper way to consider even basic modes of sub-personal consciousness is in terms of agency. This idea is not new with Merleau-Ponty but, taken together with his notion of the lived body, it is distinctive. The body orients itself in environments in terms of potentialities for it. The world is something to act in: one needs to replace the traditional Cartesian "I think" with "I can" (PP 82–3, 138).[7]

We are now in a good position to consider briefly one concept from Merleau-Ponty's unfinished work that has excited much commentary and is often cited in works of phenomenologically inspired architectural theory. This is the idea of flesh (*chair*). Merleau-Ponty uses this concept to refer to the way in which the world and the lived body are fused. In its English translation the word does not connote anything like this. Quite the contrary, one usually thinks of flesh as raw and non-experiential. In many cases, flesh is just that—i.e., meat. Part of the jarring effect of Francis Bacon's paintings of his lover George Dyer is that they hover between portraying Dyer's body as one proper to a person and as meat. This alone marks Bacon is the true father of the South Bank "experience" artists who suspend sharks in preservative or display decomposing cow carcasses in Perspex.

The etymology of "flesh" is complicated. It descends from a probable combination of Germanic and Scandinavian cog-nates that enter English in the early Middle Ages. The modern German *Fleisch* is related. But, on the surface of things, the French *chair* cannot claim any greater delicacy than its English sister. Its primary meaning is simply that part of the body that overlays the skeleton. Nevertheless, for Merleau-Ponty it is precisely the case that flesh is *not* meat. "Flesh" as a term of art just means the continuous perceptual world: to be "of the flesh" is to be either perceived, a perceiver, or both (*VI* 248).[8] What is neither perceived nor a perceiver is a kind of irrelevant chaos for him—irrelevant to phenomenology. He chooses a tactile, reflexive way of modeling how the "flesh of us" (i.e., flesh that can perceive) and the "flesh of the world" (i.e., flesh that cannot) interact: one of folding-back-upon or "intertwining." When one folds, say, a piece of fabric back upon itself the fabric becomes convoluted. Folding puts the surfaces of a self-same thing in contact with another in a way that can render the distinction between "inner" and "outer" questionable. Although it is by no means perfect, one might think that considering space in these terms yields a view where all space is topological, or even topologically equivalent. Flesh has just this structure of self-differentiation, following from the reflexive action of folding. In virtue of that structure, flesh establishes the basic terms in which one makes any number of distinctions that, if one is not careful enough, will give rise to insoluble dualisms, e.g., those of "in" and "out," "mind" and "body," "touch" and "being touched," etc. It establishes these distinctive modes of experience from within.

How specifically and less metaphorically do inanimate things figure in this picture? There are three matters to emphasize that are relevant to the embodied experience of architecture. The first has to do with the centrality of agency in perception that we mentioned above—the idea that the "I think" should be replaced with the "I can." The experience of enclosed space—its contours, lighting, texture, geometric form, etc.—is suffused by the possibilities of my perception of it, where to perceive is to engage a wide variety of bodily capacities in concert. This holds as well for objects housed within such spaces. Moving through a building is, therefore, a form of self-potentiating and, although Merleau-Ponty would not endorse the idea that there is a final stopping point for that process, of self-realization as well. Second, and relatedly, Merleau-Ponty stresses that objects and spaces appear to me almost as bodily prostheses—i.e., as continuations of my own bodily movements and aims. He holds that this is always the case, but that the experience of this bodily extendibility into space comes in degrees of depth. Because space is inextricably bound up in its perception—sometimes Merleau-Ponty unadvisedly uses the dreaded Kantian idea of constitution to discuss how essential that connection between space and being embodied is—and perception is a subtle form of "I can," all things within a perceptual field are present to me as part of a projection of my aims regarding that space and objects. They are, to that extent, extensions of my body. But there are times where the prosthetic effect is extremely strong—e.g., a musician's experience of her favorite instrument as indissolubly part of her. The third matter to emphasize builds on the other two but is home to some of Merleau-Ponty's most seemingly outlandish statements. He makes a claim that on the surface makes little sense: non-conscious things perceive us. The claim is entirely general and, thus, seems to ascribe the property "has vision" to a coffee cup. There is a way to understand this statement that retrieves Merleau-Ponty's main point less poetically. Of course, he is not claiming that coffee cups see. The point has to do rather with the possibility, already mentioned, that the structure of nature, as it is discoverable by humans, exceeds its discovery (and in some respects may outstrip it altogether). The world is perceptually inexhaustible and may even be, along certain structural lines, entirely disobliging. The image of a thing that looks back at one is one borrowed from the human experience of other beings capable of intent. Applied in this jarring way to inanimate things the analogy drives home the point that nature can be obdurate in principle and has the power to put us on the spot (perhaps the English "stare" better captures the thought).

It is time now to bank our précis of Merleau-Ponty and move into laying out some other concepts that will be important for discussing the phenomenology of architecture.

SYNAESTHESIA

True synaesthesia is where one experiences sensation of what would ordinarily be considered different sensory modalities as inherently conjoint. The modalities in question may be two aspects of one single sense, e.g., letters perceived automatically and involuntarily as colored, or may be cross-sensory, as when one automatically hears musical pitches as having color, or different pitches as differing in terms of hue or color-brightness. The immediacy and involuntary nature of the experience is key; true synaesthesia is not a matter of one thing arousing thought of another or of one modality being tripped into action by the antecedent exercise of another. The two sensory modalities are co-present within the experience, so that, e.g., the pitches just *are* colored.[9]

Psychologists consider true synaesthesia to be anomalous and even, in a sense, pathological. It is present in very few people and must be distinguished from two more common phenomena. Under the influence of certain drugs or undergoing extreme medical events such as epilepsy or stroke, one can experience certain forms of synaesthesia. It is generally not thought that these experiences trigger latent synaesthetic responses in those who undergo them; the medical or

On Architecture

drug-related stimulus instead causes synaesthetic response that would otherwise not be there at all. It is also necessary to discriminate between synaesthesia and synaesthetic-like experience. It is not uncommon for people to report that sight or grasp of an object can give rise to a palpable sense of taste: one sees the lemon, picks it up, and already can taste its juicy tang. Phenomenologically speaking there seems no reason to over-intellectualize this sort of thing and construe it as a quick and subliminal set of inferences or association of ideas. But it also does not seem right to treat these cases as truly synaesthetic: one does not inherently see the lemon, to coin an adverb, "tangily" (one sees the tangy lemon).

This scientific specification of synaesthesia should be contrasted with a more generous use of the concept in the history of the arts. The idea that the several senses are generally and intrinsically linked with one another at a deep level and allow for synaesthesia in all of us was a popular notion in eighteenth-century British empirical psychology and aesthetics. Art that could appeal to several sensory modalities at once was prized generally, and when art could do this by making the modalities co-dependent in the experience, that was counted as even better. Both Enlightenment and Romantic theories of mind on which certain aesthetic theories are based took very seriously, one might even say too seriously, the question of what kind of unity binds the various capacities of the mind together into one mind. Considering all minds as capable of at least a degree of synaesthesia is obviously a powerful way to approach the issue of this sort of unity as it applies to sense modalities. In this literature then, synaesthesia is posited as a basic condition of mind affecting everyone, and one that can be actualized in an especially potent way by art tailored to elicit the response. Today this sort of claim would be characterized as involving synaesthetic-like experience and not true synaesthesia.

Perhaps the two most famous examples of art created expressly to evoke synaesthetic-like experience are the paintings of Wassily Kandinsky and the music of Alexandr Scriabin, both cases of music/color interpolation. It seems that Kandinsky and Scriabin were true synaesthetes of this sort. Scriabin's experiments in pairing pitch with color gradation is most famously realized in his symphonic work *Prometheus, Poem of Fire*, which was intended to be performed against the background of modulating color. Calling forth similar experiences was the aim of pulsating Joshua Light Shows that accompanied the musicians at the Fillmore East in the late 1960s and early 1970s. Sound-color pseudo-synaesthesia is by far the dominating effect sought by aesthetic objects that attempt synaesthetic effects. After all, the idea of chromaticism in music is a borrowing from the realm of color, and musicians famously deploy color concepts when talking about pitch, melody, and harmony (e.g., a flatted fifth is a "blue note"). Vladimir Nabokov claimed for himself an even rarer form of synaesthesia that involved seeing letters and words as intrinsically colored. But art that sets itself about calling forth synaesthetic-like experience in virtue of the simultaneity of experience of two sense modalities is more often created by those who are not true synaesthetes, e.g., the poets Baudelaire and Mallarmé.

HAPTIC EXPERIENCE

At early stages of bodily cognitive processing, implicit experiential modalities merge with one another and their overlap can be descried as a kind of residuum present in more articulated forms of experience. Many phenomenologists have been especially interested in one way of thinking of this point of merging or overlap—what has come to be known as "haptic" experience (from the Greek verb *haptō,* = "to touch"), where vision, hearing, tasting, or smelling are deeply connected with touching. There are several different theories of haptic experience that offer distinct, and sometimes quite different, accounts of that experience. These are often conflated in the literature and, especially, in the main work of architectural theory that uses this concept.[10] I shall lay out some of the general framework for the discussion of this concept and then introduce some distinctions in order better to survey it.[11]

First of all, it is very important to emphasize that a special form of touching is at issue. The Greek on which the concept is etymologically based captures this well. The verb does not mean passive tactile contact but something more active, on the order of touching *with imparted effect.* This is an expressly intentional action ranging from subtle affecting to grasping, fastening upon, or acquiring. What phenomenologists want to stress here is that touching (in this sense at least) is, at one and the same time, receptive and active. When I type I am receiving sense experience from touching the keyboard and am at the same time and in the same action imparting touch to it. Haptic experience need not be limited to the body. Another aspect of experience that may be included under haptic experience is also very important to Merleau-Ponty and especially to architects who build with phenomenological intent. This is what one might call the experience of "extended embodiedness"—what we have already described as a kind of prosthesis. When I touch something that is within the extended ambit of my embodied experience—our prior example was a musician and her instrument—I am touching it as if I were touching myself. Touch merges with other sense modalities that are similarly extended; I needn't actually come into tactile contact with things in order to touch them haptically.

With this general background in mind it is now possible to canvass some of the views on haptic experience. Ordinarily we view touch as one among several senses. But it is a feature of many of the accounts of haptic experience that touch is prior to the other senses and perhaps, because of that fact, one might have to distinguish "haptic experience" or "haptic touch" from a more superficial sense of touch that operates coevally with the other discrete senses. One can understand the relation "prior to" in several ways, and two that are relevant in this context are: (a) logically prior to and (b) genetically prior to. Generally, again, on most accounts haptic experience is logically prior to the other senses. One particularly strong version of why this is so, which we shall turn to just below, is that haptic experience provides the logical basis for there being any discrete senses at all. A related and slightly less rigorous version of this claim is that haptic experience is logically prior to other sense modalities because it provides the structural basis for the several sense modalities to be modalities of *sense*. This is not, strictly, a claim of logical priority, but it is close to that, since the sense of priority does not have to do with the physical or embodied generation of the several senses out of one basic sense modality that is more primordial.

This brings us to the non-logical, or genetic, sense of priority. Genetic priority is this latter claim, just mentioned, i.e. that there is one, haptic, Ur-sense that experientially grounds the other senses that operate on a more superficial level. "Grounding" is, philosophically speaking, a pretty obscure and slippery notion, but it means at least two things here. First, on this picture, haptic experience accounts for the systematic unity of the senses in and through which are expressed *inter alia* phenomena like syn- and kinesthesia. Now the senses might be unified in other ways, that is, without appeal to a more basic single sense modality. For instance, they might have structural properties linking them horizontally, i.e., at the same level of operation. But many accounts of haptic experience that view it as "prior to" other more ordinary sense experience locate the unity in a more basic, grounding property of sense. There are advantages and disadvantages to this move. One advantage is that appeal to a more basic haptic sense provides a vehicle for what is shared between senses—at a higher level of sense differentiation, as it were—such that synaesthesia is possible. The haptic is both the glue that binds the several senses together and the glue that can "seep over" into the senses, so to speak, and combine them in ways that at least partly dissolve their discreteness. Perhaps synaesthetic and synaesthetic-like experiences are more haptic than their less synaesthetic counterparts. This means, of course, that something like touch will be basic to all sense experience and more express in those modes of experience where several senses figure in tandem.

Not all accounts of synaesthesia would accept touch as this Ur-sense, as I have been calling it, or even the idea of an Ur-sense at all. And this brings us to the big disadvantage of the idea that haptic experience is genetically prior to other modes of experience: the phenomenal obscurity of the experience in question. One problem for a phenomenologist with appeal to forces, processes, or states that are anterior to awareness is that they have to be modes of experience that are accessible to phenomenological analysis and not just explanatory posits. To be sure, there are some forms of what are called "non-descriptive," "transcendental," or "hermeneutical" phenomenology that loosen this restriction, but let's keep the rigorous form of the restriction in focus for now in order to highlight the problem under discussion. If the phenomenologist is going to appeal to a sense of priority of the haptic, the haptic has to make an appearance that is directly available to consciousness. One must resist, at all costs, any temptation to posit implicit, subconscious, or even unconscious experience that cannot appear to one as that experience. To do otherwise would violate the phenomenological principle that limits the application of its methodology to what appears in *consciousness*. When Jean-Paul Sartre, for instance, rejects the classical Freudian subdivision of the psyche, this is what is at stake: one (according to Sartre) cannot experience that division and the alleged interplay between the parts of the unconscious, and that means that they can only be sheer posits and are, therefore, phenomenological illicit. So, one has to establish that, if we closely attend to conscious experience, we can experience the haptic elements subtly at play. The idea here would be, roughly, that when one is seeing a rough-hewn wall of a building one is, in virtue of the touch-remnant that underlies both the content of the sight and its very possibility, sensing the "feel" of the wall.

In some accounts this share of the haptic in experience remains somewhat abstract: grasping the object or property in question and not just being a passive recipient of the experience of the property. This is often the main reason to aver to haptic experience, i.e. to reintroduce theoretically into accounts of perception the ideas that perception is active and that accounts of perception (especially vision) that enforce a presumption of essential experiential separateness between perceiver and perceived are false. But some accounts go farther than this by allowing the haptic to be part of the *content* of the discrete experiences. It is not just that (visual) perception is a grasping generally, but is also that this (visual) perception is a touching of eye to "eyed." Juhani Pallasmaa cites the infamous example of Luis Buñuel and Salvador Dali's short film *Un chien Andalou*—specifically, a scene in which a woman's eyeball is slit with a straight-edge razor in close up— to register this closeness of eye to "eyed."[12] Pallasmaa's use of the image is rhetorical and he does not really analyze its role in this regard. One might say that part of the discomfort the audience experiences on seeing the slitting of the eyeball—we all turn away at this point or, at least, have the impulse to do so—is due to the way the film destroys a sense of distance between the *seer* (us) and the *seen* (the eyeball being slit open). Destroying the eye as a real thing, and not just the notional locus of disembodied sight, is the point of the scenario.

But, to return now to the main line of discussion, one might have an account of haptic experience that is not bifurcated between two levels of experience. One might, that is, just view the sense of touch *as a discrete sense* as more powerful and informing than the other senses with which it is otherwise coeval. This would not require a distinction, as it were, between "mere" and "deep" touch at all. All one needs here is the idea of lateral dominance or priority, which puts touch ahead of the other senses and allows it to infiltrate them. This is close to the view that we all have synaesthetic experience, just at a pretty low level of admixture with touch. This is a streamlined and less metaphysical version of the view that haptic experience is prior to and part of all experience, but it also is not free from all difficulty. The main challenge will be to specify and explain what the means of lateral infiltration are and why there is the infiltration in the first place.

MOVING BODIES

"Kinaesthesia" refers to the experience of the impact of one's movement on one's perceptual array (whether interrelated synaesthetically, haptically, both, or neither). The idea is simple and has been recognized in the tradition of phenomenology by philosophers of widely divergent stripes and by empirical psychologists as well. We do not have to be very technical here; the main idea is that any account of perception, in any of its discrete modalities, has to adjust for the fact that the discrete sense modalities are located in bodies that move and thereby influence sight, hearing, smell, taste, and touch.[13] For example, in order to see, my eyes move and my head turns. Such movement and turning are not mere additions to the seeing; they are constitutive of the act and are a part of the experience of sight.

But that is not all. We sometimes overlook that muscular and skeletal positioning affect perception. Crouching over to view, say, a statue does more than merely shift my visual axis, for my visual experience is not just one of changing optical coordinates on some Cartesian scale. The way I see the statue is formed by my stature. This is a matter both of perspective and bodily compensation attendant to assuming particular postures. I see the statue as I am crouched, although one must be very careful to understand that "as" does not mean that I do two things in temporal sequence: i.e., that I first see it and then see it under an aspect. This verbal difficulty in capturing the relation of movement, posture, and perception can lead philosophers to make up expressions to describe the experience. The idea can be handled either adverbially (I see the statue "crouchingly") or, even more oddly perhaps, by concocting a compound verb (like "crouch-seeing"). Of course the idea of being in a posture or visual position that I have used for purposes of exposition is a simplification. No one is a statue.

Kinaesthesia involves even more implicit elements that impart perceptual meaning, which cognitive psychologists call "proprioception," the sense of being in or out of balance. One might think that one's being balanced in a certain way—for instance, so that one can properly ride a unicycle—is a matter of brute physiology. But there is an experience of being in balance that is usually analyzed as a function of the experience of various parts of the body being in relation to one another in an integrated way. Learning difficult tasks like riding a unicycle, skiing "parallel," or walking a tightrope, where an acquired sense of balance (or, more precisely, re-balance) is necessary, throws light on the experiential component of proprioception. Walking in the dark (or at least in pitch black) also needs to be mastered in this way. Because sight is impossible and auditory phenomena (the sound of my footfall on the wall, etc.) become more pronounced, gaining balance must be done against that new background. In a way, this is just the point made above about the kinaesthetic aspect of embodied experience with special emphasis on one of its more diffuse and taken-for-granted elements.[14]

LIGHT AND SHADOW

Much of the literature on the phenomenology of sight—even that which is phenomenologically informed—concentrates on visual form or "hard-edge" objects. There is, however, a visual phenomenon that is not comfortable with that treatment, which is nonetheless quite important to the phenomenology of art and, in particular, architecture: i.e., light. The aesthetics of light has a long history in which light is often considered in relation to other aesthetic qualities like proportion, form, linear movement, etc. A fundamental aesthetics of light—one in which light is treated relatively independently of its relationship with other qualities and as aesthetically worthwhile in its own right—is rare nowadays. But architects who practice under the phenomenological banner are building in a way that requires concerted attention to this phenomenon.

Medieval Gothic architecture had a developed aesthetics of light as an autonomous form of beauty based in metaphysical theories that conceived of light as an immaterial substance symbolizing emanating divinity. This aesthetic concentrated, accordingly, on a particular characteristic of light or, more properly, of lit objects—their luminosity, i.e., the quality of showing forth light from within.[15] Luminosity was taken to be a quality of things that directly reflected their origin in God and, not incidentally, was related to the mainstay of medieval ideas of treasure—jewels. Light as luminosity was not, therefore, primarily the optical notion of a magnitude that makes for clear appearance (i.e., well-lit conditions for seeing). Rather it concerned the emanation of truth in the profane world. The role of this idea of luminosity as truth in Gothic architecture is great. The opening up of the structure of the Romanesque stone wall to what were essentially walls of stained glass allowed the earthy composition of the cathedral wall to shine forth in divine radiance. The greatest medieval architect of light was the Abbé Suger and the greatest creations along these lines are his additions to St.-Denis in Paris.[16] His concept of uninterrupted light (lux continua) finds expression in both the narthex of the church (the entry to its nave) and in the stained glass he placed in the chevet (the choir aisle in its apse).

Architectural modernism has also prized light as an

expressive medium, but it is light without its theological underpinnings. Although luminosity can still figure in some romantic strands of post-medieval thought—one can see it for instance in the poetic imagery of the German romantic Hölderlin and the late philosophy of Heidegger—the qualities of light that guide modern architectural practice are more optically inclined. With architects who are expressly phenomenological in bent, however, more painterly aspects of light also come under consideration. Light has a different appearance depending on the color and texture of the lit surface and the transmitting medium. If natural light is in question, the quality of the light will also be seasonal, depend on the time of day, the weather conditions, its geographic source (is it northern light, western light?), etc. One way these effects are often discussed is in terms of the "color" of light. For Suger, color was provided by the stained glass, but white light can also have apparent hue depending on the factors listed above. A "bluish" light may be a result of a certain degree of sunlight relative to the aperture and the nature of the reflective surface inside the building. Of course these effects are also present in exterior aspects of architecture.

With light comes shadow and its cousin, darkness.[17] Shadow and darkness also admit of degrees and colors, as anyone who has experienced the difference between nighttime darkness and true pitch blackness can attest. Shadows are complex phenomena every bit as rich in their experience as the light that calls them into being. Part of the difficulty in talking about the experience of shadow comes from the relation of shadow to its dual sources: light, with its own phenomenological richness, and the thing that casts the shadow. Part of the difficulty stems from considering shadows as ontologically secondary to the objects that cast them. It is easier to talk about bounded figure than the dispersed after-effect of the conjunction of object and light. Nevertheless, shadow is constantly in play in architecture. Indeed it is hard to think of a more complex and rewarding art of shadows than architecture. Not only is this because there are multiplicities of shadows in a process of constant change throughout the day and year in a given building, it is also because a shadow creates what one might call "light-edges" at its borders, which edges are in continuous play with other linear aspects of the building structure. Light and shadow allow a building fixed in its line and plane to shift its geometry and much else through the course of days and seasons, transforming itself as an object of spatial experience through time.

EMBODIED ARCHITECTURE

As a matter of principle, it is possible to talk about any architecture in terms of its being an object of embodied experience. Such a general discussion would be a bit chivying: it would be one in which many buildings might be assessed in terms of the concept, yet be judged as falling short of providing a rich and varied field of such experience. This is for the simple reason that most architects do not have the aim of providing such an environment, although they cannot help but do so to an extent. For these reasons, it is much more rewarding to discuss the topic of the embodied experience of architecture in connection with specific examples of architects who bear fully in mind the phenomenological impact of their buildings. For a large part of the remainder of this chapter we shall discuss the work of an architect who has built in full awareness of embodied consciousness: Steven Holl. We shall concentrate on one project of Holl's, the recently completed Block addition to the Nelson-Atkins Museum in Kansas City, Missouri (2004).[18]

Holl is not the first architect to write and build with the importance of the spatial experience of the body in mind. Focus on the ways bodies relate to architecturally enclosed space is as old as the first systematic writings on architecture. But the approach that Holl takes—explicitly relying on Merleau-Ponty—is an example of something quite different from the run-of-the-mill in this area. It is quite true that modern writers on architecture have generally allowed that accounting for its role in experience must take one beyond the form or look of a building, past its design, and even superseding the reference that buildings have to one another. Even the conservative philosopher and art critic Roger Scruton devotes a good deal of energy to develop an account of imagination and spectator variation relative to given architectural form (almost always illustrated by classical patterns and façades).[19] The problem with such accounts is that, first, they tend to treat *design* as a basic trigger for the experience of architecture, rather than one of many ways to undergo that experience; and second, they operate with an idea of imaginative variance that is not closely enough allied to the idea of a lived body. One might think that architectural modernism, guided variously by the great Chicago architect Louis Sullivan's motto "form follows function,", would be an improvement. Adolph Loos' sloganeering against the "crime" of ornament in buildings was certainly meant to clear away from the space of architecture matter that he took to be inessential and even obfuscating to the proper unity between space and movement in it. But the concept of function as one finds it deployed in the canonical work of high architectural modernism is only as good as the concept of experience to which function relates. How *do* humans function in functional architecture? There have been complaints on this score that mainly come down to the charge that high modernism is inhuman in its concept of function. Some of these anti-modernist criticisms, to be sure, are blatantly pre-modern and do not engage charitably or subtly with the main claim of architectural modernism: that buildings can reform human-ity. The anti-modern complaint runs: humans are what they are and buildings have no business messing with that.[20] Other more moderate critics of architectural modernism, while tolerant of the notion that buildings might have a proper role in extending human experience, argue that most modern buildings have in fact not done so.[21] But even if one grants the main contention of the moderate critic of architectural modernism—that modernism has been largely insensitive to the lived context of buildings—that is no argument against the view that modern buildings can pay proper heed to their experiential impacts. Past practice, even if longstanding and consistent, is no proof that modernism and experiential sensi-tivity cannot coexist. That would require a demonstration that the constellation of concepts that make up "architectural modernism" are, as a conceptual matter, incompatible with the idea of such sensitivity. No one has even tried to prove that. In fact, it turns out that a certain strand of modernism not only can provide a platform for phenomenological rich-ness but may provide the only one currently possible.

In his writings, Holl develops a vocabulary to describe the way in which he takes architectural space to be structured. Much of his terminology is adapted from Merleau-Ponty and late-period Heidegger. The basic term is "intertwining," which is a cousin to Merleau-Ponty's "chiasm." Holl uses the term in two distinct ways. The first describes the interrelation between what he calls "ideas" and "phenomena."[22] An idea, in this context, is the overall concept that governs the plan of the structure, as that concept guides the building process. The idea is "limited"; it is not an absolute and unyielding plan that determines the building come what may. Rather it must be responsive to the specific demands of the site and its phenomenological potential. Holl calls this potential "phenomena."[23] Although he can seem sometimes to view an idea as an indeterminate representation of the overall intent of the planned structure, at other times Holl adopts the much more interesting notion—developed out of Hegelian resources— that an idea is a *process* of the realization of an initially under-developed core set of aims. Ideas and phenomena fuse, then, in the process of the building itself. One might even say that the idea just is the building. Second, Holl sometimes uses the word "intertwining" to refer, not to a relation between idea and phenomena, but rather to a relation between phenomenal elements—that is, between various elements of potential experience through which the idea is realized.[24] An example might be where perceived embodied movement interacts with light, color, and structural texture.

There are two further concepts that play central roles in Holl's architectural theory. The first we have already discussed at some length: that haptic experience is primary. Holl seems to hold that touch is horizontally fused with the other sense modalities. Crucial for him is the marriage of sight to tactility; he seems to hold that this passage is opened through increased visual acuity.[25] Perhaps what Holl means is not that increased acuity of vision as a representational faculty is sufficient to engage explicit haptic awareness (i.e., seeing in more detail) but rather increased experiential attention to the way touch infiltrates sight. The second additional concept that informs Holl's architectural thought and practice is "parallax." Parallax is the effect of point of perspective on the relative apparent position of two objects. It is overwhelmingly a visual concept, but it might be translated into other perceptual modalities. So, for instance, I see from the point where I am standing in an art gallery a statue and its background wall. As I change my position, I will see the object against a different background, and my relation to the two objects, as well as their apparent relation to one another, will alter. Add to this two further ideas: first, that my movement will be continuous and thus so will the alteration; and second, that "the point where I am standing" is just conceptual shorthand for an embodied perspective. That means that my eyes are at such-and-such-height, at this-or-that angle because of the tilt of my head, even that they are rotated in their sockets in a way connected with meaningful proprioceptive potentialities—all points we have considered in our discussion of kinaesthesia. "Parallax," as Holl means it to operate, tokens a continual and continuous flowing experience of shifting sight planes and rearrangement of the visual field—what Holl often calls "viscosity" in order to pick up the haptic element in such an experience.[26]

Within the scope of this book, I cannot hope to provide an adequate discussion of the Bloch Addition as a whole. It is a very involved work and will repay repeated study in years to come. We can only focus selectively on the building in order to show some of its attention to the embodied experience of it. In that vein, let's begin discussion of the Bloch Addition with the idea of parallax in hand. It is possible to enter the Addition in many ways, but all of them will lead you to a central lobby that is the point of connection between two broad, gently sloped ramps, one leading upwards and one downwards in the same direction. The downward slope leads back to the museum gift shop, which is tucked discreetly under the upward slope. The wall material is a polished plaster and the passages described by the slopes are bathed in light from various source angles and transmitted through various glass treatments. When I noted the effect of light on the flooring it was 1 p.m., October 20, 2007, there was a bright blue sky outdoors, and the light was northerly. It is important to be specific. Holl builds by keeping firmly in mind the effect that changes in season, and differences in time of day and the direction of source can have on the quality of light. The main source of light in this passage is skylights. The floor of the downward slope is hand-troweled, dark granite and glass terrazzo, which is slightly uneven and which thereby imparts a sense of aqueous movement to its surface. The upward slope is composed of a compound angle with a rise of twelve degrees and a slight tilt at its midway point away from axis. A view from the base of this upward slope illustrates Holl's use of parallax in the building and the resonance of that use with his emphasis on other phenomenological qualities of the interior structure (Figure 1.1). As one walks up the ramp, one is drawn up into the building, as it were, by shifting points of perspectival resolution composed by the plane surfaces and the way in which light models them (Figure 1.2).[27] Walking up the compound slope puts one's balance a bit off-center and reinforces ever so slightly the off-kilter feeling of perspectival irresolution. The experience is both richly pleasurable and uncanny. If one steps back from the experience a bit to think of such things, the experience can lead to a criticism of standard ways of handling such a space in which a multiplicity of resolution points are not given. A lobby usually affords one the first

Figure 1.1 Main Lobby, Nelson-Atkins Museum [Roland Halbe Fotografie]

experience of a structure. This one, right off the bat, teaches us something about both movement relative to embodied spatial perspective and how architectural space generally might respond to such movement.[28]

As well as being the main entrance to the contemporary wing of the museum, the lobby and its ramps are literally the linchpins of the building. But let's step back from it to consider some of the unifying elements of the museum as a whole. The Bloch Addition comprises five structures in all—which Holl refers to as lenses—with above-grade lighting through both skylights and a U-plank system that integrates two layers of channel glass. The glass is sandblasted, translucent, and provides a measure of passive solar heating. Embedded between the panels of glass is a complex lighting system that engages at dusk. This allows a seamless transition

Figure 1.2 Main Lobby-Atrium, Nelson-Atkins Museum [© Andy Ryan]

between the lenses' light-transmitting and holding capacities during daytime and their luminescence at night. Sheets of what Holl calls "vision glass"—that is, transparent glass—are placed at discrete intervals at grade to provide a connection to the existing Beaux Arts main museum building and the copious sculpture park that surrounds the Addition. The lower four lenses serve to display the modern and contemporary art collection of the museum. They are situated relative to one another in a step-wise descending pattern, modeled to the slope of the land towards the fronting street of the museum property; the lenses dip in and out of the grassy knolls in which they are embedded (Figure 1.3).

The black terrazzo floor is continued throughout the space that comprises the four galleries. The plan allows for two main modes of access to them. First, one can simply move from gallery to gallery, that is, through the exhibition space.

Figure 1.3 Aerial View, Nelson-Atkins Museum [Timothy Hursley]

This is typical of many museums of course, but Holl directs traffic here in innovative ways. Each gallery space has its own unique play between natural and artificial sources of light that both serve the displayed art and the experience of the space as such. Ceiling treatments are varied geometrically in subtle ways to modulate the bodily experience of moving from one gallery to another and within single spaces. Of special interest are the treatments of the so-called T-walls that hinge lens to lens. The vaulting of these hinges receives more and more complex geometric treatment as one moves through the structure as a whole, allowing for an accumulating sense of the complexity of how the spaces are interconnected at their pinnacles. The eye and body are drawn up into the height by means of expressions of both structural and experiential interest. This effect is supplemented by infusions of mixed northerly and southerly light by what Holl calls "flutters"— T-walls that are open at the top and flanged so that it is possible to mix in different ways south and north light. It is crucial that none of these architectural pyrotechnics comes off as such—i.e., that they do not call attention to themselves and subvert interest in the art on display. A good part of this receding authority of the building is due to the way Holl places the complexities of the architecture in a deeply haptic realm. Almost every experience of the structure of the museum is reinforced by shadings of material texture, light, color, etc. (Like Cézanne's late watercolors, Holl weighs objects against color.) Because Holl typically achieves his architectural aims by reinforcing the embodied experience of the building by drawing from a whole range of phenomenologically enriching sources, and not by means of grandstanding statements anchored merely in optically oriented geometric structure and form, the building serves the art it houses or, better, to which it is a home. Put another way: if the vocabulary in which an architect's innovation is expressed is limited to "structure," as modern architecture often understands the term, she will have to work big—big architectonic gestures on the order of a Libeskind. Sometimes such buildings can be wonderful, but they are not typically multidimensional. Holl can build big—the Bloch Addition is quite sizeable—yet work small. Mies van der Rohe famously said "less is more"; perhaps smaller is bigger too.

The second way into the galleries is via a descending ramp that runs from the lobby area in the opposite direction of the more assertive ascending and descending ramps that form the main lobby space (Figure 1.4). This ramp runs to the side of the galleries, ending in an indoor sculpture court that houses a collection of Noguchi sculpture. Although I say that this access ramp is "less assertive" than the other two ramps that form the architectural spine of the building—the other two ramps more fully engage parallax than does the descending access ramp—the descending ramp is hardly without phenomenological complexity. It is best appreciated, I think, from its lower base, standing just prior to its emptying out into the Noguchi court. The gentle wave of the terrazzo floor continues from the lobby, but its connection with light is altered to emphasize the intimacy of the galleries. Holl has cut away narrow rectilinear forms in the ceiling at various angles to the walkway, which forms emit light that the dark floor does not so much reflect as soaks in and diffuses. This effect ties together the floor and ceiling elements more proximally than is the case in the lobby, with the result that the ramp—which is, in fact, a very large structure—is imbued with a kind of meditative stillness. The ceiling light is mixed with traversing side light and the subtle molding of the wall has a

Figure 1.4 Gallery Ramp, Nelson-Atkins Museum [Roland Halbe Fotografie]

similar effect on the "holding" of the light as does the floor of the ramp.

When one experiences the Bloch Addition to the Nelson-Atkins one has an achieved appreciation of the way the whole structure hangs together as a kind of architectural climate or mood. As we said previously, Holl's effects do not hit you over the head: you have to pay attention to them to get them. The complexity of the architecture does not operate at an overtly intellectual level—at least not initially. Rather, it engages a number of perceptual capacities, native or learnt, and, at the same time, encourages their further appreciation and development. We'll return to the museum later in Chapter 3 to discuss its exterior and its relation to its site, but even if we restrict ourselves as we have to its interior, the fidelity of the building to Holl's stated principles is clear and convincing. The Addition is suffused with intertwining in both senses that Holl emphasizes. Its features are mutually phenomenologically reinforcing: light, structural form, and material work together to realize an organically structured and perceptually rich work. Moreover, the idea of the work that, through the building process, results in the Addition, is receptive to the demands of specificity of its material components and to the particularity of possible experiences of the building. It would be a mistake to think that the work does not represent or express a very strong forming idea that it carries to fruition, but having a strong overall plan for the project does not mean that the idea dictates in the abstract the process of its realization. One of the things that is so striking about Holl's work is its sensitivity to itself, similar to the way that being sensitive to oneself and one's relation to one's particular life paths is thought indicative of humans. No one, except maybe Kleist, the political philosopher John Rawls, and a few plan-addled architects, think that you have to have a single well-scripted, overarching and unified "life plan" to lead a meaningful existence. Buildings often seem to be fixed objects, more like geological formations than poems. And so they are, if one attends merely to their physical properties at the expense of all else. Holl all but prohibits this. One could, I suppose, hunker down and walk through the Bloch Addition resolutely ignoring the complexity it offers to bodily perception. But that would be to miss what the building is all about and to misunderstand its nature.

ARCHITECTURE AND EMBODIED CHANGE

Holl's work in Kansas City is the present-day *summa* of architecture built in light of phenomenological ideas concerning spatial embodiment. Part of the richness of the building involves the potential it sets forth for a variety of experiences within it. Having these potentialities at hand can by extension suggest that what one takes to be the standard modes of being embodied are not exhaustive of the phenomenon. In turn, this may suggest that there may be new, as yet uncharted ways of being embodied. Can architecture push the envelope on the limits of embodied experience? Some architects think so and build accordingly, almost experimentally. Holl's museum extension of course can change our capacity for embodied experience by virtue of deepening our experience and understanding. But does Holl believe that architecture can actually change embodied existence by changing the basic capacities for such experience themselves?

What would it mean to change capacities for embodied experience and how could architecture have that as an aim? As we have seen, being embodied is not coextensive with "having a physical body" but particular capacities for being embodied would seem at least to supervene on what kind of physical body one has. That is, if the physical bodies of humans were sufficiently different, different possibilities of embodied experience would be present. So, for instance, if humans had webbed hands or prehensile feet, certain kinds of grasping would be impossible and certain other modes made possible. Infrared vision would open up a range of experience while shutting down another. Perhaps over the long term, being in certain types of buildings, like being in certain natural environments, could change biology through adaptive response. But, in the short term, capacity change through biological change does not seem within the ambit of architecture.

So, the question of whether architecture can change experience by changing our basic capacities for experience will turn on the degree to which humans, as they are presently constituted biologically, have latent and underutilized capacities. Put another way, the question will involve how much plasticity humans have as embodied agents. But being plastic enough to sustain a significant change in capacity is only half the story. Architecture would have to bring to the table a sufficiently rigorous and different set of experiential prompts to push the capacity in question into change. There might be many ways to conceive of how this push would be provided, but one that has firm roots in art practice in the twentieth century is to introduce radically different and even shocking experiences to both dislodge us from routine ways of experiencing things and to induct us into new experiences. The idea that art should be a matter of severe disorientation has a provenance in the visual arts in Dada and in the literary arts in the form of the language poetry movement.[29] Add to these sources the Zen Buddhist practice of meditating on kōan—verbal forms that serve to break down conceptual barriers to enlightenment—and you have the beginnings of understanding the architecture of Arakawa + Gins.

Arakawa + Gins call their architecture—when they call what they create "architecture" at all—"procedural."[30] The procedures involved are tightly scripted ways in which their buildings force embodied responses to them that are radically non-standard. Arakawa + Gins deploy a very intricate vocabulary to capture the basis which embodied change can occur. "Landing sites" are the basic preconditions for human awareness, often proprioceptive or otherwise pre-conscious activities. They are ways in which one finds oneself immersed in the world perceptually. Arakawa + Gins reserve the term "perceptual" to aimed intentional forms of consciousness, while they call "imaging" those landing sites that are aware in more diffuse ways of the background that supports the intentional object yet remains untargeted by directed consciousness. "Dimensioning" landing sites are instances of consciousness of relative position of things within a given "surrounding" environment that take into account both the discrete awareness of objects within the perceptual field and the imaging of indeterminate parts of the field: "A chair as pictured or held in place by perceptual landing sites (direct perception) with the assistance of imaging landing sites (indirect or imitative perception) has for its perceiver a distinct position in relation to everything else in the room—the work of dimensionalizing landing sites (part direct, part indirect perception)."[31]

Although the vocabulary is new, it is clearly aimed at expressing a relation between the experiential field—what Arakawa + Gins call a "surround"—and a perceiver in which the perceiver "creates" her own embodied space in response to architecture. This idea should be familiar—both Merleau-Ponty and Holl endorse versions of it. But Arakawa + Gins build structures that are meant as "hypotheses" to test how far one can distend experiential categories without them breaking down entirely. As one might imagine, building architecture that aims at frustrating experience in order to extend it is not going to be very lucrative. Commissions for experimentation through building are hard to come by. Arakawa + Gins have built fairly extensively nonetheless. Most notable perhaps is their 1995 Site of Reversible Destiny— Yoro, located in Gifu Prefecture, Japan (Figure 1.5). By means of radically shifting terrain both internal and external to the main buildings, fashioning structural elements of the buildings that require reversal of schemata for up and down, left and right, and other forms of regularized orientation, and many other devices that introduce ambiguity into parallax and other means of visual orientation, the Site of Reversible Destiny became a tremendously popular destination—a kind of theme park for architectural challenge or an anti-Disney

Figure 1.5 Elliptical Field, Site of Reversible Destiny [Courtesy Arakawa + Gins / Architectural Body Research Foundation]

World. But putting embodied experience out of balance through architecture is, in this case, not an end in itself. The guiding idea is to open up new ways to experience that follow upon an initial disorientation. Whether and to what extent this is possible is speculative, as Arakawa + Gins recognize— that is one reason why they call what they do "hypothetical." That destiny be reversed need not be thought of as a reversal of time; "destiny" is what is fated to be, and it is this idea that we are fated to remain within the ambit of given everyday embodied experience that is the target of their work. In some of their moods, it seems that Arakawa + Gins want to cease thinking of architectural space in temporal terms, as is often done within phenomenology.[32] This can give the impression that they believe that passing through a sufficiently reorienting architectural space can hold time at bay. The point is that taking space itself as a primary way to form embodied experience will encourage development of more radical spaces to move through—ones that are not antecedently ordered according to preconceived ideas of how one ought to pass through them.

Procedural architecture is, in some ways, more ambitious than architecture that is attentive to phenomenological issues of embodied experience. Holl's Bloch Addition intends the transformation of those who experience it, but the transformation in question is one involving increased attentiveness to and use of standing modes of embodied experience. One deepens oneself within the building and that is change enough. Procedural architecture does not build upon and extend awareness into basic modes of experience. It subverts normalcy in the hope that standard categories of embodied experience will be replaced with new ways to experience the world spatially. It can be profoundly disorienting, requiring the experience of radically non-standard architectural spaces and, in order that that experience be critical, a linking up of it with the "ordinary" by way of memory and imagination, where the possibility to remember the old is always threatened by the novelty in question. Sometimes proceduralists write as if the experience itself is critical. That seems unlikely. The Dada shock effects that Arakawa + Gins' "extreme architecture" draws upon require this juxtaposition of the known and unknown, but the critical impact would be very difficult to register while one has the shock experience. Moreover, one might also think that circulation between disorienting spaces would breed an inability to react to them subtly, a diminution in response and awareness of the surroundings. Or, perhaps these objections are just impressions taken by those of us who have not had the requisite reorientation. At this time, there is no telling what impact procedural architecture will have. In the meantime, buildings like Holl's that deepen given responses rather than sweep them away might appear richer and more enabling.

CODA: NON-ARCHITECT ARCHITECTURE

In this chapter I have been discussing in the vernacular of Merleau-Ponty's phenomenology some quite highly developed examples of architecture. By "highly developed" I don't just mean "highly evolved" or "really complicated." I mean buildings that are built with explicit theoretical awareness behind them. In our case, the awareness in question has been phenomenological. These buildings, perhaps for the very reason that they are explicitly theoretical, if not theory-driven, may seem so *sui generis* that I seem to run the risk of isolating the importance of a phenomenological approach to them. This would be bad for a phenomenological approach to architecture because it would greatly limit the domain of its possible application. It would be bad for non-architect buildings because it would stipulate that they could not exhibit phenomenological richness. And because if there is an ethical dimension to the anti-formalism of the phenomenological approach to building—an issue for Chapter 3—there would be a form of ethical life that would also be up for grabs that ordinary buildings might not share.

At the outset I said that any building can be the subject of phenomenological assessment. This is in many ways a trivial truth—so long as a thing is a perceptual object, it can be treated phenomenologically. But it is also non-trivially true. All architects build with some appreciation of the perceptual nature of buildings and with some idea of how they are to be lived in; the kind of analysis that we have been pursuing in connection with Holl and more experimental forms of architecture will have its place across the board. I have chosen Holl and the experimentalists because building with phenomenology explicitly in mind is apt to produce the most complex realizations of experiential space, and discussion of those, in turn, provides the best illustration of the importance of the phenomenological approach to understanding architecture. "Advanced" buildings will be those that push us the most spatially and that means that, if what one is after is great richness of experience with the possibility of extending one's awareness of one's embodied potential, the architect-buildings are likely to be the ones that are most important.

How realistic is it to expect non-architect architecture to explore phenomenologically rich building practices? Not very, I'm afraid. Although there is no conceptual barrier here, it is plain truth that challenging buildings are very, very expensive. Many of their effects are due to non-standard materials, custom lighting effects, and non-orthogonal walls, ceilings, and floors. This does not put them out of the category of domestic architecture per se—Wright achieved some of his effects by these tailor-made means—but it does price them out of the ordinary, especially now that the modernist Prefab movement is all but dead.

Two

From the time of Attic Greece, theoretical disciplines concerned to evaluate cultural practices have recognized architecture to be important. Just what made it important, and how to categorize it, however, have changed a great deal over time. The Greeks used a word, *technē*, to group together activities that had social value as skills to be passed on from generation to generation. Plato develops an understanding of *technai* in which there is the requirement that a skill have a *logos*, a "rational structure" of which one can give an "account" (the Greek word *logos* can mean both things). That is, for an activity to be a skill it has to be something that has elements that can be singled out, related to one another, and taught. One needn't have a theory of such a skill in order to possess it, but one needs to know enough about its general structure to be able to pass it down. The Greeks took architecture to be such a skill, but so were wheel-making, throwing a spear, and raising oxen. This idea that there is nothing especially fine about architecture or other arts that shows them to be inherently higher forms of human endeavor than, say, engineering, persists into Roman times and beyond. Although there are important differences between the Greek attitude towards *technai* and the Roman towards *ars*, they are both reasonably covered by the English term "skill" and not "fine art."

ARCHITECTURE, THE POOR RELATION

The idea of the fine arts, as well as that of a body or system of them, is a modern invention.[1] Given that religious architecture was of such importance in medieval and Renaissance life, one might think that, once one had the concept of fine art in hand, architecture would have not only a clear claim to be an important art but even a preeminent one. The experience of the arts—art, music, painting, and literature—was at that time confined to the aristocracy. Churches, on the other hand, were centers of life for European communities from every social strata and all but defined the ethical life of the age on a daily basis. This point has not been lost on later architectural theory. Ruskin resurrected this ethical function of medieval architecture—and of the so-called Decorative Gothic—as a bulwark against what he took to be soulless modern architecture.[2] In a slightly different vein, the French architectural historian Viollet-le-Duc saw a modernized form of medieval building as a remedy for what he took to be the stodgy complaisance and clubby exclusivity of the Beaux Arts. In fact, however, the humanistic theoretical disciplines in the West up through the nineteenth century consistently rated architecture at or near the bottom of the fine arts in terms of significance. Philosophy has been a leader in this field. Precisely when something like a domain of the "philosophy of art" or of "aesthetics" emerges in the thought of the German rationalist A.G. Baumgarten and others of his generation, and especially with its true systematization as something like an autonomous intellectual discipline with Kant, architecture takes it on the chin when it comes to measuring up against the other arts. There are very complex reasons why this is so, and explaining the low status of architecture, once truly philosophical accounts of the arts are available, can say as much about philosophy's bullying about the arts as it does about the arts themselves. But some generalities are admissible.

The main difficulty with architecture relative to the other arts as far as philosophy is concerned can be tracked along two dimensions. Both have to do with unstated presuppositions central to the philosophy of German Idealism dominant at the time when philosophical hierarchies of art became prominent. At what one might as well call the metaphysical level, architecture comes up short because it is the most material art. What being a material art entails is not entirely clear in this tradition, but for simplicity's sake let's begin by asking if "being material" might just mean "being a physical object." This doesn't rule out much. Daydreams cannot be material in this sense, but even music, often taken to be the least material of the arts, requires sound waves. More proximate to architecture, paintings are physical objects, as is sculpture. So are poems, at least if one takes them to require being written out. Clearly, being a physical object is insufficient to mark architecture off from the other arts (or much else); something must be added in order to differentiate one from the other. Perhaps emphasis might be laid instead on the mass or size of architecture relative to the other arts. Perhaps "material" means "massive." This too is a matter of degree, of course. In the later eighteenth and early nineteenth centuries no other art works were as large as architecture. This is not merely to say that no non-architectural work was as massive as the Basilica at St. Peter's—one of the favorite examples in theories of art of that time—that so outstrips other works in size that one's experience of it is more in the order of the experience of a natural event, like seeing a mountain or a great storm, than seeing a painting. It is also to say that most domestic dwellings are larger and more encompassing than the grandest of historical paintings. But it is not just spatial displacement that is being flagged here; rather, it is spatial displacement plus the tectonic solidity of the building. Take any Romanesque cathedral. Not only is it huge, but one experiences in its thick stone walls and masonry an implacable structural solidity seemingly rooted in the earth. Heidegger thought Greek temples, or at least select ones, had this property as well. Some writers, Schopenhauer and Hegel most prominently, took the thought farther, eschewing description of massiveness of architecture for description of it in terms of what they took to be the abstract metaphysical forces that underpin it. Schopenhauer expresses the thought in an especially vivid way: architecture's nature lies in a tension between (a) the "downward impulse" of the]force of gravity inherent in the mass of stone or other building material and (b) an "upward impulse" of the space that the walls of buildings describe by enclosing and "shaping" the space.[3*] Hegel, who builds social dimensions into his assessment of the relative value of architecture, is a bit more accommodating.[4*]

Whether the idea that architecture is essentially material makes sense or not, one might still wonder what is so bad about being material in the first place?[5] So what if architecture is an art of solid, gravity-bound products? One historically influential idea was that the more material an art form is the less intellectually engaging it is. There is a popular idea today that intelligence, or at least the most valuable kind of intelligence, has to do with abstract thought—mathematical ability, game manipulation, and certain aspects of musicality. Of course this is only one kind of intelligence, and it is difficult to avoid the impression of intellectual self-regard in lionizing the idea that intelligence should be equated with abstract thought. Perhaps intellectuals or technocrats are deeply suspicious or envious of experience, with which abstract thought needn't (though it might) have much to do. Notwithstanding this, in the period that we are discussing, few thinkers had theories of the significance of art that *directly* stressed abstract thought. Rather, the theories were "aesthetic" and, thus, had to do in the first instance with giving an account of the provenance and operation of art on the human capacity to feel, not think. Even so, it is characteristic of these theories at this time that the feeling that was held to be specific to the experience of art was either a result of or closely related to the exercise of conceptual thought—being either a precondition to such thought or a more unfettered exercise of it. Idealist theories of how humans think stressed a central role for mental representation. This role was imported generally into aesthetic theory and, specifically, into the hierarchical ranking system of the arts. There is much debate about what a representation is for these German philosophers—some of their individual theories coincide or overlap with one another, others do not. It is, anyway, unclear how the concept of representation would play a primary role in accounting for architectural meaning. A building does not usually "stand for" or "mediate between" itself and something else. Chartres just *is* Chartres, whereas Velasquez's paintings of the Spanish royal family are *of* or *about* them, and the marks on the page of poetry collectively represent words which in turn represent something else. Of course buildings can represent or refer to other things, perhaps other buildings even, but the idea is that they are not inherently representational. What is bad about that, according to these philosophers? Because buildings are non-representational they cannot support the exercise of human imagination, a facility required in a whole range of basic cognitive endeavors, the exercise of which provides a special kind of pleasure—one that awakens and intensifies the sense of one's overall cognitive vocation. Even Hegel, who more than other idealists stressed the ramifications of social life on art, takes a representational relation to art on the part of a culture as a whole to be a mark of cultural maturity.

The view that representation is definitive of the higher arts, ironically perhaps, puts architecture in the company of one art that is thought today to be almost definitively "abstract," i.e., instrumental music. The second-generation idealist Schelling is most aware of this, writing in 1802 that architecture is a kind of "frozen" or "concrete" music (*erstarrte/ konkrete Musik*).[6] He means by this that, just as architecture is an art whose purest realization comes in the construction of the spatial relations between its parts, or even of space itself, music is an art for which temporal relations (rhythm) are essential.[7*] Whether music is representational at all is a question that surfaces now and again in the philosophy of music. At first blush, the answer seems obvious: it certainly *can* be. To take some well-known examples discussed by the philosopher of music Peter Kivy, Arthur Honegger's *Pacifica 231*, Handel's *Clock* Symphony (no. 101 in D Major), or the finale of Tchaikovsky's *1812 Overture* sonically represent, respectively, a locomotive, a cuckoo-clock, and cannon salvos (in some performances the latter *are* salvos using blank shells). Such musical effects always run the risk of trying one's patience, seeming coy or even childish. In any event, this kind of representation is a very small part of music-making (such tricks would not have any more place in rock music or jazz than they do in art music as far as I can tell). We don't characteristically expect or especially like representation in music, and that is probably because not only does music not require representation, but the experience of musical representation counsels against it, at least if "representation" means something like "sounds like." But of course "representation" is a pretty broad concept and the idea that it primarily means "being an imitation of" is probably based on an overwrought analogy between music and visual experience. Humans do generally orient themselves by means of sight, sizing up objects for handling, judging distances, differentiating one thing from another, etc. The idea that representation means similarity springs from this idea. But the "world" of music is not this sort of world at all, and in the world of music other types of representation can and do predominate.[8] Regardless, the sorts of representation pertinent to instrumental music are not pictorial, distinguishing music from painting (two-dimensional spatial representation) and sculpture (three-dimensional spatial representation). Of course, painting is, in fact, three-dimensional—canvas and the paint on it have physical depth. But the point is that painting, relative to sculpture and architecture, has to *achieve* its pictorial depth by perspectival techniques. Music is time-dimensional only, and whatever representational qualities it might have are limited by that fact, so it was argued. This put music, like architecture, on a far end of the representational scale. Its capacity for abstract representation—to have one's cake and eat it too—places it above the pictorial arts in much the same fashion that architecture is placed below them, i.e., because they are not crafted to resemble other things.[9]

The second conceptual level at which the hierarchy of the various arts functions involves an issue that is also ultimately related to the question of materiality. The theories that have so shaped the history of systematic philosophical thought about the place of architecture relative to the other arts developed precisely at the time when there was an emergent middle class with a recognizably bourgeois set of attitudes about moral, political, and social values. The American and French Revolutions had taken place; the socialist revolts of 1848 had not. The academics who proposed these schemata—and this was also the first generation of philosophers whose main job it was to teach at universities and compose their works in "vulgar" languages—were for the most part middle class and promoters of radical ideas like democracy, capitalism, and an end to aristocratic privilege. To people so given over to work and earning as the prime indicators of the good life, the pleasure of art became a pleasure of leisure. There are actually two sides to this phenomenon. On the one hand, work under most conditions is laborious and freedom from it, with the time to enjoy other things, is pleasant. At the same time, given enough success, one might approximate the free time that a noble once enjoyed and imitate the nobility's characteristic modes of enjoying it, among which art is counted. It was especially enjoyable for the upper nobility to commission art that reflected well upon its taste, and if one were truly rich and fortunate, art in which one figured as a subject. The same was true of bourgeois art. So, for instance, in an intimation of what was to come in Europe more generally, Netherlandish portraiture becomes an extraordinarily important marker of this class. These two aspects—respite from labor and pseudo-aristocracy—go hand in hand. What this means for the hierarchy is that arts are also rated along lines of greater and lesser involvement in human industry or in terms of their remoteness from everyday affairs. Kant's aesthetic theory is replete with this idea—traveling under the banner of what he calls "disinterest"—so much so that even basic conceptual work (problem solving, over-attention to the conceptual structure of the world, etc.)—substantially impinges on the experience of beauty.[10*] The shift to the concept "beauty" here is not a throwaway. Beauty, at least at this point in history, fairly means reflective detachment. Too much concern wrecks the kind of free, rapt contemplation that tokens the best engagement with art. This idea of disinterest carries the day through the main philosophers of art of the period, with the exception of Hegel. Schopenhauer is perhaps the most insistent. He ups the ante on Kant by taxing art, and particularly music, with enabling one to escape momentarily at least from the suffering endemic to living at all, by sloughing off the representational and bodily preconditions that necessarily give rise to the suffering. Schopenhauer's casting music as the metaphysical emancipator is revealing. In his thought the two strands of the hierarchical idea we have considered come together as if meant for one another: the asceticism of abstraction and the aestheticism of non-instrumental thought.[11] Architecture does not show well on the metric of disinterest. Buildings are used for all manner of purposes—business, political functions, homes, sporting events, social gatherings, etc.—and, indeed, many buildings are built specifically to such dedicated uses. One might be so impressed by the pragmatic side of architecture that one might deny that one could be successful in abstracting from one's consciousness these pragmatic elements of buildings, leaving at best a hybrid version of the contemplation necessary for a heightened experience of art.[12]

So, the treatment of architecture by philosophy relative to the other arts has been rather harsh. Even the greatest accomplishments in the field pale next to a Raphael Madonna and child, a Beethoven sonata, or a sonnet by Shakespeare. Things have changed of course, as we are no longer wedded to idealist philosophy (some of us never were!) and do not need to accept the presuppositions that led it to rate architecture so poorly. Even so, the place of architecture within the arts is by no means a simple question, nor is it an issue that one can just ignore. This is because architecture nowadays plays a central role in the presentation and structure of non-architectural art works. Moreover, ideas that have developed in architecture—most notably ones of architectural space—have gained currency in other arts. Let's first turn to some examples of architecture as a context within which other art is experienced. At the close of the chapter, we'll turn to issues of architectural influence upon the content of other arts.

ART IN ARCHITECTURE: THE MODERN ART MUSEUM

Any architect will tell you that an art museum commission is a plum assignment. There is tremendous status involved in building a museum, especially if it is in a major city with a famous art collection waiting for a new home. It is easy to understand why architects compete so ferociously for these jobs. Cities consider art museums to be among their most important cultural assets. I don't use the term "assets" lightly; apart from the desire to have a great building as a home for a great collection of art, museum buildings themselves have become discrete travel destinations, reasons for tourists to come to a city and spend money. In the 1960s airport terminals were hotbeds of architectural competition and part of the reason for that was the advent of the Jet Age, when the very idea of flying from Europe to America in seven hours was stylish. No one would want to reduce Saarinen's great terminal building for Kennedy Airport in New York City to a matter of style (architects are allergic to considering their work under fashion categories), but to deny that sleekness is part of the concept of the building as well as what the city sought to project by building the terminal is to beggar history.

Museums have been around in various forms, public and private, for centuries, but the modern idea of a grand art collection that is open to the public can be dated from the time of Cosimo de Medici's commission to Vasari for the building of municipal offices (*uffizi*) in Florence in the mid-sixteenth century. Retaining the name of its original purpose, the Uffizi gallery became stocked with Medici treasures, artistic and otherwise, and was open "to the public" by special appointment (and permission). Other museums were built with the intention that they be public, for instance the Museo de Prado in Madrid, built by Carlos III as part of his attempt to render a grand municipal space, or meadow (*prado*), that compared to Paris (Carlos was a Bourbon). The first museum dedicated to art and only art is the Hermitage in St. Petersburg, in which Catherine the Great housed her recently purchased trove. It "opened" in 1764, but access was severely restricted, a fact that is registered in the name of the collection. Catherine wistfully commented that none but she and the mice had seen the abundance she amassed there (the museum was made truly public in the October Revolution). The collections that form the core original holdings of many great European art museums were the private property of kings and queens of course. In America a similar structure prevailed, substituting robber barons for real ones. The Louvre, the Hermitage, and the Belvedere were all royal residences or galleries and only later were they true museums. If what one means by a "public" museum is one open to all without special permission or class restriction, the Louvre, opened in 1793, can be counted as the first.

As is reflected in Vasari's design of the Uffizi, the idea that galleries or museums demand architecture befitting their contents is not exactly new. In the mid-twentieth century, however, there developed an attitude toward the display of art in museums that seemed to compromise or curtail the effect of dramatic architecture in the museum. This development has come to be known derogatorily as the "white box" view of gallery construction. The white box is a neutral, right-angled display space that is designed to isolate art works from any assertiveness that the architecture might work on them. Its emphasis on off-white, rectilinear spaces processing in predetermined directions that suit the chronology of the displayed art makes for a common space in which one will find it very difficult to exploit the interaction of embodiedness and architectural surround that we discussed in the first chapter. Vasari's Uffizi is a good example of what was to be avoided, according to the white-boxers. Vasari was a painter, an architect, and a substantial theorist and practitioner of what was then the cutting edge of perspectival design. The outer galleries of the Uffizi represent his painterly concern with perspective—they are narrow, very long, and accentuate the geometrical volume of the hall to the point of competing with the paintings hung there. But it was not Vasari who was most in the mind of the advocates of architectural neutrality in the museum. An even better example of the perceived danger is Frank Lloyd Wright's Guggenheim Museum in New York (Figure 2.1).

The museum, located on the Upper East Side of Manhattan on 5th Avenue between East 88th and 89th Streets, directly across from Central Park, was commissioned to house an estimable collection of modern art works—mostly sculpture and painting—owned by the Guggenheim family. The collection was started by Solomon Guggenheim, the wealthy industrialist

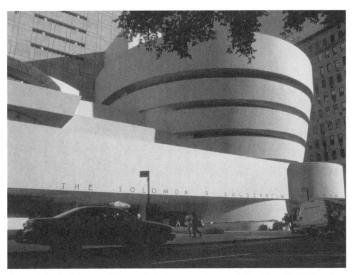

Figure 2.1 The Solomon R Guggenheim Museum, New York City, New York [The Art Archive / Neil Setchfield]

for whom the museum is named. Guggenheim's collection, amassed in the 1920s and 1930s, comprised several important works of key early twentieth-century Middle European painters—especially Kandinsky and Paul Klee (Guggenheim had visited Dessau, where Kandinsky and Klee taught). At first this was a private collection, housed in Guggenheim's suite at the Plaza Hotel. Guggenheim's niece, Peggy, was an important art collector in her own right. She established a museum of sorts in 1939 in midtown Manhattan and later, in 1942, opened her famous gallery, "Art of this Century." Post-war abstract expressionists like Pollock and Rothko formed the center of this exhibition. The Elder Guggenheim's artistic advisor, the painter Hilla Rebay, approached Wright to design a permanent home for his holdings (with some of Peggy's on loan) in 1943, ostensibly because he was in her estimation the most "advanced" American architect.

From the start it was a controversial design, different in many ways from the iconic "Prairie Style" domestic designs that had earlier made Wright's name. Even the structure for which Wright is perhaps best known—the house Falling Water in Bear Run, Pennsylvania, constructed just seven years prior to the commissioning of the Guggenheim—was not immediately indicative. His most famous commercial project, however, the Johnson Wax Administration Building in Racine, Wisconsin (1936–9), begun at the same time as Falling Water, was. The Johnson Wax Building first shows Wright to be operating with the curved, molded concrete forms that were to figure so prominently in the exterior of the museum. Wright's architecture had used concrete cantilevers inter-preted in tree or plant form before, but the Johnson Wax Building was an expression of Wright's "organicism" in structure-bearing form like no other.[13] The huge atrium that is the main working space of the building is supported by 30 foot (9 meter) tall mushroom-like pillars with the charac-teristic rounded edge that can be seen prominently in the Guggenheim (Figure 2.2). The shading afforded by the play of light on the curved forms adds to the impression that they are natural forms. One can make the argument (and Wright, who carefully developed his own cult and with it the idea that his work as a whole was one, seamless thing, certainly made it) that the plant-form that had become structural in the Johnson Wax Building was but the logical extension of the plant and other organic motifs that had played a role in non-structural ways (in masonry, etc.) in Wright's earlier domestic projects. This can be traced back to the Chicago architect Louis Sullivan, in whose offices Wright interned,

Figure 2.2 Interior of Johnson Wax Building, Racine, Wisconsin [© Artifice, Inc. / Artifice Images]

who used such motifs in the façades of many of his projects. It is by now part of the canon that Sullivan, like the Austrian architect and theorist Adolf Loos, eschewed "decoration" and, if what is meant by that term is "merely ornamental" figure added to the structure, that seems right. It would be wrong, however, to lump Sullivan and Wright together with Mies van der Rohe and Le Corbusier on this issue. While the latter pair fought ornament in the name of Platonic form, the former did so in the name of beauty.

The exterior of the Racine building is also revealing. Just as with the Guggenheim, the Johnson Wax Building's exterior expresses the molded curve of its interior in a way not dissimilar from the Art Deco resort architecture that one finds now nicely preserved in the South Beach section of Miami Beach, Florida. (Just in case one balks at this comparison, let me add that Wright wanted to paint the exterior of the

Guggenheim pink.) The effect of the lights in the night view is especially important, just as in the Guggenheim exterior, lighting is perceived as a recessed band that is as much a part of the solidity of the structure at night as are the banded walls. Simply put, the Guggenheim exists in the same object-realm as does the Johnson Wax Building. Instead of mush-rooms, we have a conch-shell, whose upward spiral is expressed in both the exterior molding of the façade and in the interior walkway and gallery space. The museum's main space is an atrium around which is wound an inclined walk-way. In the original main exhibition space, the walls are adjacent to the walkway, which is otherwise open to the atrium above and below (Figure 2.3). This means that display of art works is always on walls whose surfaces are at least slightly curved. Moreover, the action of walking the slope puts one at a skewed body angle to works when one stops to

Figure 2.3 Lobby of Guggenheim Museum, New York [Corbis]

look at them. Add to this the slightly vertiginous feeling of having the wide-open atrium at one's back and it adds up to a unique museum-going experience.

To put it mildly, the Guggenheim Museum is an assertive building. Wright took great pains to design it to elicit, through the experience of moving in the space itself, a calculated set of responses, which are due to the architecture alone. Of course, he was designing a *museum* and part of the intended response is had by looking at works in this architectural context. But many have found that the art is almost secondary to the response—a mere trigger for it. More to the point, some have found the building to be so assertive that it oppresses the art within it. This was found so much to be the case that an additional, more art-friendly and orthogonal gallery space was added in the 1990s. I lived in New York City from the late 1980s to the mid-1990s and visited the museum often. There was one show that struck me as hung well, that is, it seemed to fit in the museum. This was an exhibition of Frank Stella paintings, whose geometric muscularity and physical presence could hold their own against the architecture. I suspect others have experienced other exhibitions in the Guggenheim that they felt were fruitful. But it is, I believe, undeniable that exhibiting art in the main atrium space is quite difficult and that this difficulty is due to the nature of the building. It seems almost as if Wright wanted to make things as hard as possible for what he might have considered the "ornament" of art in the pristine architectural space. Perhaps he would have liked the museum to be empty or as nearly so as possible, in order to better appreciate the building itself as art. The idea is not as far fetched as it might seem at first. Daniel Libeskind's Jewish Museum in Berlin was opened for visits prior to any installations and many found it a more powerful experience to be in the empty building than to be in it with the exhibitions present. This is *really* saying something, since many of the exhibitions have as their theme the Holocaust. Empty museums don't always work this way of course. When I lived in Atlanta, Georgia in the 1980s it was something of a standing joke that Atlantans had spent their hard-earned civic dollars on a marquee museum by Richard Meier (which, by the way, echoes a lot of Wright's Guggenheim design, albeit antiseptically) with nothing to put in it. The museum, by itself, was not worth it.

This theme of museum versus art is especially pointed just now. But the phenomenon of art housing other art is not new. Medieval cathedrals were and are such art, but they are not museums and their overarching purpose—to express and induce the experience of humanity's relation to divinity—does not put their architecture into competition with the art that they contain. Painting and statuary in a church—not to mention music—is given a context in the environment and was made with that context in mind. No medieval artisan would have complained about domineering Gothic arches! Modern museums, however, don't have that context at their behest. They developed as places in which to experience art that, increasingly through history, was made with the intent that it could stand on its own merits—indeed, must be seen as stringently autonomous. There is a story that Peggy Guggenheim had asked her protégé and sometime lover Jackson Pollock to make a painting that she could hang in the foyer of her East Side apartment. For whatever reason there was a miscommunication about the size of painting needed and the finished canvas would not fit the space. The painting in question was one of Pollock's flung-paint works, a style of painting that was at that time synonymous with high individualism and post-war art world self-confidence. Marcel Duchamp, the Dada artist who was a taste-counselor for Guggenheim and who made the "ready made" infamous, suggested a simple fix: saw off the offending remainder. This solution was, of course, entirely in keeping with Duchamp's own artistic practice, but seemingly not with Pollock's. After all, how much more assertive and inventive would two more feet of painting be! But Pollock allowed the surgery and the foyer wall won.

The Guggenheim is now an international collection of museums. The umbrella organization, the Guggenheim Foundation, surely may be said to commission and collect its museum buildings as art just in the way that it has a core, standing collection of paintings, sculpture, and video works. Under the entrepreneurial stewardship of its recently departed director Thomas Krens, the museum has not been shy about the architecture of its other branches. Most famous is the Guggenheim Museum in Bilbao, Spain (Figure: front cover). This museum, with its titanium-clad, gull-winged exterior and cavernous interior, built by the Canadian-American architect Frank Gehry, is quite probably the most instantly recognizable building of the last quarter-century. Gehry has said that, when he was drafting the plans for the museum, he had very specific ideas about the art that he would like it to contain. More precisely, he has said that he had the monumental rolled-steel sculpture of Richard Serra in mind. Of course Gehry's museum does not dedicate itself to Serra's works, as a museum on a smaller scale (e.g., the Musée Picasso in Paris and the Warhol Museum in Pittsburgh) might devote itself to the oeuvre of a single artist. But Gehry's statement does reflect a certain attitude towards what works might best be shown in the museum, which, more than perhaps any other museum of its vintage, *shows itself* in the bargain. Such work would be monumentally large, non-figurative, metallic, and shaped geometrically in a way that echoes the undulating curved arcs of the building's famed roofline. Serra's works are shown there and, by all accounts, are shown very successfully. Does the Guggenheim Bilbao devour its art the way, say, Goya's Saturn does his children? However the cases sort out, it doesn't seem to matter to the popularity of the museum. It is striking that a work that is by consensus a seminal modern building has so enthralled visitors who aren't, presumably, so modernism-minded. So captivated are they that the museum has single-handedly turned its host city into a vacation destination, when once it was a down-at-heel regional post-industrial town. One might go there to see Serra's works in the way one visits the Alte Pinakotek in Munich to see the Rubens, but the overwhelming impression is that people go to the Bilbao museum to go to the Bilbao museum. Not many museums can claim this distinction; in fact, not many buildings can claim it. The Guggenheim strategy for the "global museum," where holdings are moved around from location to location, is predicated on having "destination architecture" in place to receive them. The museum building does the main work of attraction; the art inside is a bonus. Although this idea is freshly minted, well postdating Wright's involvement with the Guggenheim Foundation, one can see an anticipation of the view that, to put it crassly, "if you build it, they will come" in the sea-shell on the Upper East Side.

I mention Richard Serra's rolled steel sculptures in connection with Gehry's Guggenheim museum as an example of how an architect might build with the intent that what she builds is closely related to another kind of art, or even art made by a specific artist. But some of Serra's work—i.e., his massive steel works—raises other interesting questions for architecture. Specifically, Serra's work poses the question of what differentiates architecture from sculpture. Sculpture and architecture each have their individual histories, but they also have a joint history of their relation to one another. Up until fairly recently, it was not difficult for anyone to tell whether an object was one or the other. Nowadays there is sculpture of such scale and form that architectural categories may be thought to apply to it. As an artist, one might start out more or less "doing sculpture" and find that one is tending towards more architectural forms or ideas. The reverse might be equally true.

A 2007 retrospective at the Museum of Modern Art in New York City covered many stages of Serra's very substantial output but—for me at least—the centerpiece of the exhibition was an installation of his rolled steel work. The installation covered an entire floor of MoMA and consisted of three sculptures: *Sequence, Band,* and *Torqued Torus Inversion,* all made in 2006. Each is a very large work—12 ft 9 in by 40 ft 8 in by 65 ft 2 in ($3.88 \times 12.40 \times 19.86$m), 12 ft 9 in by 36 ft 5 in by 71 ft 9.5 in ($3.88 \times 11.10 \times 21.88$m), and 12 ft 9 in by 36 ft 1 in by 26 ft 6.5 in ($3.88 \times 11.0 \times 8.09$m) respectively—fabricated out of 2 inch (5 cm) thick weatherproof steel. Sculpture is often distinguished from painting in terms of how many spatial dimensions it is able to represent: in the case of painting, two dimensions (height and width of the canvas or other surface) and in the case of sculpture, three (adding depth). Physically speaking, it has always been known that this way of distinguishing the two arts is radically false: painting is three-dimensional too—canvases, etc. have depth. In the history of modern painting, artists variously accentuated this fact by building up paint on the surface (e.g., van Gogh); by using techniques to show depth by breaking down representational paradigms of painting that used perspective to create a "false depth" that occluded the physical depth of the painting (e.g., Pollock); or by building out from the canvas sculptural elements by affixing objects to it (e.g., Robert Rauschenberg). This is to say that there is a difference in the history of art between being three-dimensional and representing objects three-dimensionally. If Hegel and others are right, sculpture nonetheless had to fight its way out of something like two-dimensional representational paradigms to assume the role it is taken to have had as three-dimensional art that represents in three dimensions. The idea of free-standing sculpture around which one can move and, in so doing, "take it all in," is what Serra's large-scale work operates against, however. Serra's rolled steel works demand that they be moved through and not just around, as one might other forms of sculpture. His work is intended to create a bodily, and not merely an imagistic, experience of it by crafting an overall environment in and through which one moves. This sounds like architecture, or even phenomenologically astute architecture.

What's more, the three Serra sculptures that formed the core of the MoMA show educate bodies that traverse them by upsetting, sometimes subtly and sometimes not, habitual ways of perceptually orienting oneself in enclosures. The walls of all of the sculptures describe arcs that change their pitch and surface regularity as one moves through the pieces. There is enough height for the walls to seem to enclose and to focus one's equilibrium in terms of the shifting contours of the walls, their relation to one another, and the path that their bases describe on the floor. In particular, *Band* confounds expectation by making ambiguous what the exterior and the interior of the piece are and how they are related (Figure 2.4). *Band* is a kind of experiential loop that expands out from and then folds back into itself. *Sequence* achieves a similar sort of disorientation by nesting two long, rolled forms in an S-shape (Figure 2.5). Several of the openings are experienced as structural occlusions, yielding access to more interior spaces and, thereby, intimating that those spaces are hidden or secret.

When I visited the exhibition on a weekday in late summer

Figure 2.4 Richard Serra, *Band* [© 2008 Richard Serra / Artists Rights Society (ARS), New York]

Figure 2.5 Richard Serra, *Sequence* [© 2008 Richard Serra / Artists Rights Society (ARS), New York]

2007, the floor on which all three works were grouped was teeming with young schoolchildren on a field trip. After an initial period of barely contained order brokered by three docents, the children began gleefully to run in, out, around, and through the three sculptures. They were twisting their bodies in this way or that, sliding on their knees, oohing and aahing as they looked upward from supine positions to better appreciate the vertiginous immensity of the walls— they were quite obviously changing their bodily visual orientations in order to play with the structures. "Play" is not a throwaway term. Some art calls for engaging very basic human capacities, ones that are often collected under the rubric of "imagination," for playing—for taking a thing and, with fewer limitations than might be imposed by more work-aday sorts of objects, doing things to and with it. There are several interesting and intricate accounts of something like this capacity for play in the aesthetics literature—the work of Richard Wollheim on "seeing-in" and of Kendall Walton on "mimesis" would be examples—but for now I would stress something that those accounts downplay (Wollheim is better on this point than is Walton): that play is a social category and a bodily one as well. One can of course play by oneself, but this is a little like the philosopher Ludwig Wittgenstein's famous analysis of so-called "private language." Even when playing by oneself one plays, ordinarily, in such a way that another is implied—either by expressly taking on the role of another or by other means. The point is this: play is a social activity, something humans do together, that is imaginative and whose point amounts to nothing more or less than actualizing those social capacities. Play is fun, an often ignored but very important social and aesthetic category.[14] And this play of course implicates the body. No one can watch children play with any real understanding and miss the importance of bodily mimicry, modeling, etc. to the activity. The raucous play of the children on that day in MoMA stood out against the rather more formal consideration of the art by the worldly grown-ups at the show, most of whom were suitably clad in New York black-on-black and the latest in architect eye-wear. It seems to me that the kids had the better of the occasion.

Of course there is other large-scale work that involves tweaking experience in ways that are recognizably phenomenological. The artists of what the critic Rosalind Krauss has called the "California Sublime"—Robert Irwin and James Turrell—seek such effects via their work.[15] Turrell is an especially interesting case from the point of view of the confounding distinction between architecture and art. His work has been driven towards larger and larger architectural structures as ways to elicit experience by the idea that the more all-inclusive such structures are the better their perceptual effects are realized. (In Chapter 3, we shall see that this is a version of an idea that is often at the forefront of architect-centered urbanist theories.) Through uses of diffused light, point of sight leading from room to room, and subtle shifts in color saturation and perceived depth by the use of scrims in some of these installations, Turrell's smaller-scale work (which is still often on the scale of a room or rooms) is extremely difficult to categorize. Some of its intent and effect stems from Turrell's expertise in sensory deprivation and saturation experiments and from an exploration of the effects of various filtered textures of artificial light on the experienced physicality of structures. Many of his most compelling works of this sort—e.g., *City of Arhirit* (1967) and *Wedgework III* (1969)—instill in the viewer-participant a womblike, yet ambiguous experience of not knowing where to go or what, specifically, to look at, that serves to make the very act of going or looking a more explicit part of the experience than it would otherwise be. One might also call this bodily displacement "uncanny" (*unheimlich*), to use Freud's term for a very special late nineteenth- and early twentieth-century version of the sublime: there are markers of familiarity but also of something being askew. *Wolf* (1984) is a prime example. What binds the work together is a concern with the substantiality of light and with the purity of experiencing that substantiality in a trancelike state. This is an idea one finds in music as well. In the musical practice of the Drukpa Kagyu sect of Tibetan Buddhism, chanted pitches and their timbres are related to an Ur-vowel that is a sonic basis for all things. Singing variants of this vowel brings on a state of extreme non-objectual concentration, moving the singer close to primordial non-individuation.

I said that Turrell has been driven to create larger and larger structures for his experiments in heightened bodily perception. The largest, and the project that has claimed most of his attention over the past thirty years, is his *Roden Crater* (1977–). Inspired by his experience as a pilot, his somewhat Zoroastrian ideas about light as an autonomous source of meaning, and his interest in Zuni ideas concerning the inter-twining of time and light, *Roden Crater* is the *non plus ultra* of Turrell's art. It is a work of what one might call "found archi-tecture." The crater in question is an extinct volcano located on the periphery of the Painted Desert in northern Arizona. Turrell's interest in using the volcano as the basis of a work in which light and space could be experienced as conjoined in various non-standard ways was, it seems, rooted in the idea that the isolation of the crater allows for a central observation point from which to experience a subtle palette of natural daylight on and inside the structure of the volcano, as well as an experience of the deep darkness of the astronomical sky that allows for a heightened appreciation of very old light, i.e., light that has its origins in stars many millions of light years away. Particularly interesting to Turrell is the mixing of these two types of light—old and new—at dawn and dusk, and its effects on the experience of space. Turrell has excav-ated various parts of the interior of the volcano and provided access to exterior light sources via shafts. Several chambers not only allow for the effects of light on the spaces that are enclosed; they also reflect celestial movements on the floors or walls. One might see this as Turrell's adaptation of an idea most familiar from the organization of Roman cities, where the settlements radiated out from a consecrated center point

(umbilicus).[16] This point, as the etymology betrays, was identified with what was considered to be the center of the human
body, the navel. But the point was also cosmologically central
and it was this centrality that gave rise to the idea—prominent
in much classical thought—that the body is a microcosm
on a structural par with the universe at large. This architectural *cum* sculptural concern with bodily expression and its
cosmological place marks Turrell's work throughout.

I close this section by considering an even more direct
relation between architecture and sculpture in an artist's
work. The American artist Gordon Matta-Clark is known primarily through his so-called "building cuts." Matta-Clark
would scout buildings scheduled for demolition or for auc-
tion or seek willing participant-owners of such buildings,
and acquire permission to alter them by cutting through
them. His work dates from the early to mid-1970s and has
often been equated with sculptural minimalism, earth art, or
Situationist happenings. Although it is not exactly correct,
as it is sometimes claimed, that Matta-Clark was a forgotten
artist—many artists from the downtown New York movement of that time cited him as an important influence and his
work has been the subject of major retrospectives—it is true
that he has not assumed his proper place in standard histories
of late twentieth-century art. It is easy to see why Matta-Clark
fell through the cracks—to pun poorly. Because much of
his most interesting work was done with buildings and other
objects that no longer exist, his work in a real sense also does
not exist. Now, the fact that Matta-Clark knew, accepted,
and even embraced the imminent demise of the objects that
underlay his work has led some art historians quite naturally
to stress the importance to him of the ontological imperman-
ence of art generally. To those more inclined towards critical

social theory, emphasis has been laid on the way Matta-Clark's work reflected on the nature of detritus or ruins in contemporary consumer culture, particularly the decrepit state of New York City in the 1970s. Or perhaps Matta-Clark is concerned to critique the "tear it down to put it up" culture of modern land speculation. It has even been suggested that his work is a general criticism of the activity of architecture, construed as a hegemonic discipline bent upon erecting inappropriate and insensitive buildings at the cost of their environments. Matta-Clark did sometimes call his work "anarchitecture" and was himself trained as an architect in what were then the rather strict rationalist confines of the Cornell University School of Architecture.[17] (Matta-Clark's father, the Surrealist Robert Matta, had worked for a time in Le Corbusier's atelier.) Still others have seen Matta-Clark as a large-scale sculptural minimalist.

It is not wrong to see all or some of these various connections at work in Matta-Clark's art, but focusing on one at the expense of others can mislead. In particular, the sculptural comparison with minimalism is subject to this caveat. The art-historical reception of much of minimalism was shaped initially by the influential work of the art historian and critic Michael Fried.[18] Fried argued that much minimalism was a product of attempts by modern sculpture to compete with theatrical display. The stark, thing-like character of minimalist art, according to Fried, forces upon one an explicit awareness of one's being conscious of the object, which defeats what he calls "absorption" in the work. Fried thinks this is a bad tendency in contemporary art, one that shifts art away from its proper concern with defining its essential components, allowing for deeply subjective and perhaps even ethical experience.[19] The upshot of this, historically speaking, was to focus almost exclusively on minimalism's activity of questioning standard notions of what the concept of art means, especially in the arts of painting and sculpture. To understand Matta-Clark in this way is to place in the foreground issues of "destruction" as an aesthetic category at the expense of the phenomenological experience of his work. For, if Fried's diagnosis of minimalism is on target and can be extended to Matta-Clark (the latter is something that Fried does not consider), there may not be a substantial phenomenological dimension to the work that is worth talking about.

Another distraction from the phenomenological—and architecturally phenomenological—aspects of Matta-Clark's work is the idea that he turned away from architecture as a vocation. In some sense this is right: he did not build buildings, he "unbuilt" them. But there is a facile and a more sophisticated version of this claim. The facile version is that Matta-Clark's building cuts were rejections of architecture *tout court* by destroying its products, i.e., the buildings that were cut apart. A slightly, but only slightly, better variant of what I am calling the facile view is that Matta-Clark's cuts were celebratory intimations of the buildings' imminent demise (at least this variant captures the fact that the buildings which Matta-Clark transformed by the practice of his art were already goners). But Matta-Clark's own artistic practice puts the lie to both versions of the facile claim. He was extremely interested in documenting for futurity the process of cutting the buildings, the experience of moving around in them after they were "finished," and the general form of life of the cohort of artists in the downtown scene who variously supported his work. He did this through film and photography, sometimes his own and, at other times, by enlisting the help of fellow artists like the photographer and filmmaker Robert

Frank.[20] A more sophisticated version of the assertion that Matta-Clark "unbuilds" buildings is that this activity is an *extension* of his architectural training and relies upon architectural activity for its realization. Part of the Cornell curriculum at the time Matta-Clark was a student was an application of the idea, developed most thoroughly in the early Bauhaus, that architects should learn other arts and crafts as integral parts of their education. Matta-Clark's training in sculpture emerged from just this kind of artistic cross-training. There is no testimony on his part and nothing one can glean from his work to suggest that this learned continuum between sculpture and architecture was not part of whatever countercultural transformation he was undergoing. On the contrary, his drawings for projects, sketches, and works on paper bear witness to an abiding acceptance and reliance upon architectural thinking and practice—albeit unconventional thinking and practice—in the realization of his projects. In particular he was interested in grafting the process- and materials-oriented approach to art "events" of the contemporary scene onto a phenomenological approach to the experience of his manipulated buildings that does not end him up too far from Turrell.[21]

Fried's analysis of theatricality and absorption has not gone unchallenged. Rosalind Krauss has deployed aspects of Merleau-Ponty's phenomenology of the body to understand minimalist art. Most important for her is the concept of "all-overness" demanded from many minimalist works. Her claim is that such sculpture eschews both the dichotomy of figuration and abstraction and forms of viewing the art work passively. In virtue of the fact that minimalist works resist standard ways of seeing art in terms of representational or expressive function—because such works insist on being of the world rather than *about* it—the viewer is forced into an awareness of her own motility relative to the work and of the fact that any one viewed aspect of the work always intimates other aspects under which it can be experienced.[22] Krauss is perhaps less concerned than she might be about why exactly an art work's being of and not merely about the world would force embodied response to it in this way. Her view, while critical of Fried's disapproval of the forced response (Fried's is the kind of objection Rousseau would have liked), is really very much like Fried's when it comes down to how the effect is forced. Substitute for "theatricality" the formula "insistence on embodied self-consciousness" and the accounts are quite similar.

Krauss has briefly considered Matta-Clark under this phenomenological rubric,[23] but the art historian Pamela Lee applies the same insight more directly and extensively to Matta-Clark's work without subsuming it wholesale under the category of minimal art. Matta-Clark's concern was to render his "found architecture" in such a way that traditional ways of experiencing boring orthogonal buildings were replaced by surprising and challenging architectural surrounds. He was concerned with the counterpoint of odd geometrical forms to bodily orientation and disorientation, as well as with the effects of natural light on color and shadow in the structures. He also aimed at certain syn- and kinaesthetic effects, mostly involving the reciprocity of the tactile and the visual.[24] To be sure, one should not discount the fact that the way he rendered his buildings was by dislodging their structures and accentuating their raw materiality. None of the cuts is surgical; they are meant to be rough. So, there is a kind of pre-demolition that Matta-Clark is practicing relative to the ultimate fate of these works (and the buildings on which they are based).

But even though in a sense the work lives in the past subjunctive, in another sense it doesn't. Depending on whether one wants to count the photography and filming of the making of the work as simply documentation of the work or a proper part of it, the work may survive, and intentionally so. I was fortunate to be able to see a retrospective of Matta-Clark's work at the Museum of Contemporary Art in Los Angeles (MoCA) in fall 2007 with a good friend, who has a knowledge of contemporary visual art that far outstrips my own and an eye to match (it is always a good idea to go to exhibitions with such superior creatures!). Two things in particular struck us. One I have already mentioned—the palpable joy in community that the video conveyed of Matta-Clark's world of artists. This was not so much of a surprise, as it underscored what we had already known. What stood out, though, was the precedence of the photography over two other components of the work—the films I just mentioned and even some of the remnants of the cut buildings that were on display. One might have thought, if one were convinced that Matta-Clark's work was essentially mournful, that the building pieces would have been the most powerful objects in the exhibition. But they were surprisingly banal, more mere documentation of what happened than were the photographs. There was a time in his life when Matt-Clark exhibited the detritus of the buildings in museums proximate to the still-existing buildings that were subject to being cut. So, perhaps it is not altogether fair to relegate the remnants of the cut structures to the category of what is left over after the art is done; perhaps they too are part of the work. Regardless, their relative lack of interest did not hinge on this ontological nicety. It was rather due to the overriding need for us to imagine being in one of the structures. This the photographs revealed, if only as a tantalizing after-effect of the experience. The most striking of these were photomontages that are akin to Cubist bricolage, as the art historian Thomas Crow has noted.[25] These were assembled by Matta-Clark precisely to convey an after-the-fact simulation of the experience of disorientation of being in the building. They are not so much referential, then, as they are expressive. One of Matta-Clark's most complicated cuts and one of his last projects, Circus (1978), can serve as an example. A simple documentary photograph can give a hint of how phenomenologically complex the experience of moving through the building must have been once Matta-Clark had cut it (Figure 2.6). But, placed beside the montage photo of the same, which attempts to express that complexity, the other photo pales (Figure 2.7, right). Most architects are wary of photographic depictions of their work and very choosy about which photographers they will use. This is because photographs are both the most likely way people encounter famous architecture and so are very important to its cultural reception, and because a photo cannot do justice to the complexity of perceptual interactions with the building. Matta-Clark's use of photography is much more integral to the architectural intent of the work than an illustration in a book might be. Instead of giving in to photography's limitation as a medium for experiencing buildings, his photographs attempt to use the means relevant to photography to give an analog of the architectural experience, without of course trying to fool us into thinking that they are adequate measures of what it was like to be in the buildings. Of course, the photographs can stand on their own as art works, but to sever them from their causal origin in the project of actually cutting the buildings is to miss their full import.

Figure 2.6 Gordon Matta-Clark, from *Circus* or *The Caribbean Orange*, 1978 [Museum of Contemporary Art, Chicago, black and white documentation photograph / © 2008 Estate of Gordon Matta-Clark / Courtesy the Estate of Gordon Matta-Clark and David Zwirner, New York / Artists Rights Society (ARS), New York]

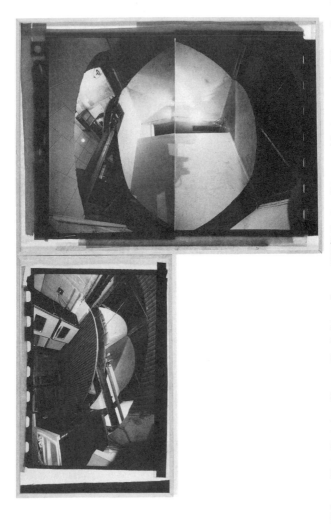

Figure 2.7 Gordon Matta-Clark, from *Circus* or *The Caribbean Orange*, 1978 [Collection of Museum of Contemporary Art, Chicago. Restricted gift of Mr. and Mrs. E. A. Bergman and Susan and Lewis Manilow / Photography © Museum of Contemporary Art, Chicago]

ART IN ARCHITECTURE: SOUND AND SPACE

Nowadays music is by far the art with the most cultural heft, especially given the possibilities of downloading, ripping, and streaming that the internet affords. IPods alone have revolutionized both the pervasiveness and the experience of music. There are many arguments to be had concerning whether this is a good thing or bad. But whether it is good, bad, or a mixture of both, the explosion of music from the drawing room or front porch into the public sphere (even if IPods do give a sense of being cut off from the public as well) has left architecture a bit in the lurch. Much at the same time as public museums began to develop, the modern experience of hearing live music in groups—what we usually call "going to a concert"—emerged. It is true that the advent of recording technology impacted this: one could hear the Metropolitan Opera broadcast on radio, listen to Caruso on the Victrola, or hear the latest pop recordings on 45s. The advent of the LP record was seen by some to usher in a real threat to concert-going, and CDs and, especially concert DVDs, might be thought to have even greater impact. In the world of Western art music (what is often called "classical music") concert attendance is markedly compromised, especially in the age range that one seeks to cultivate to ensure future ticket sales: youth. Moreover, with the evolution of the modern recording studio—an environment that cossets musicians in a dark, womb-like world of seemingly infinite sonic possibility— artists like the Beach Boys and the Beatles all but gave up touring in favor of the control of the recording console. It would be wrong to lay this shift only at the feet of the pop musicians, however: the Canadian pianist Glenn Gould was ahead of them in his retreat into the studio, as was Vladimir Horowitz before him.[26]

Music venues are of course quite diverse, from the smallest jazz clubs to formal concert halls to large athletic stadiums where major rock acts play. Although not quite on a par with museum work, building a concert hall—most likely to be used for art music concerts—is a prestigious assignment that is apt to cause an architect to operate at full throttle. Earlier in this chapter we mentioned Schelling's idea that architecture is "frozen music" in connection with the peculiar status that architecture and music have in a hierarchy of the arts that is biased towards visual art and the associated concept of figurative representation. Music and architecture stand as mirror images to one another at opposite ends of the spectrum where representation descends or ascends into the twilight of non-representation. But how do music and architecture relate to one another in buildings that are made in order that music be heard in them? Does or should architecture stand as a "frozen" analog to music in such cases? Or does or should architecture think of music as its "liquefied" self—some of Bruckner's symphonies might come to mind or, even better, the late work of the composer Morton Feldman?[27]

What is Schelling getting at with the idea? Is it a species of metaphor, where two unlike things are thought to be similar in virtue of a third thing that connects them? Or is the idea a kind of metonymy in which one term is substituted for another? It seems to me that the notion that architecture is frozen music is rather complex. Most scholars who have thought about the equation have understood it ahistorically. A guiding thread, and one that we have mentioned before, might be that architecture is an inherently formal spatial art just as music is an inherently formal temporal one. When one translates or understands a spatial art in terms of a temporal one, the former will be rendered in temporal terms as static, and thus, figuratively speaking, as "frozen." On this view, the real conceptual work here is done by a presumption concerning the relation of pure space to pure time. Putting matters in this way is fine, as far as it goes. But there is no one set of ideas in human culture about the nature of space, time, or their relation to one another. One has to ask, then, what did an early nineteenth-century German intellectual think about the nature of space, of time, and of their relation?

Art theory at the time that Schelling makes his statement was in flux. The intellectual scene in Germany two generations prior to Schelling was dominated in the arts by the neo-classical theories of Winckelmann and their influence had not completely died out by the time that German Idealism was in its nascent form. Winckelmann understood the role of classical art in his contemporary context to be one of reforming and integrating what were seemingly disparate and certainly diffuse elements of German "culture" (Kultur), which enjoyed what coherence it had in virtue of a common language, rather than a well-formed national character. As usual German art theory and literature were at least a half-century behind the cutting edge on this point. France had already had its neo-classical moment and come out of it. For the study of architecture, "going neo-classical" meant thinking in a Vitruvian way. As we have seen, Vitruvius was not insensitive to the role of the body in architecture. Indeed, much of his theory revolves around the idea. The size, shape, and form of a building are, according to Vitruvian principles, directly related to the geometric interactivity and proportions of the idealized human body. The problem with Vitruvius' formulation, and those variants of it that controlled the Renaissance idea of architectural proportion and regularity, is not that it ignores the human body altogether. It is rather that the idea of proportion from which one extrapolates architectural regularity is impoverished. Its organizing idea of proportionality is merely geometrical. Put in Merleau-Ponty's terms, Vitruvius operates with an object-centered conception of what phenomenologically is a non-objectual experience. Modernism inherits a version of this problem. Le Corbusier's idea of the bodily "resonance," as he puts it, in architecture is limited by this object-centered view with the difference that, unlike Vitruvius, Le Corbusier puts his point in terms of the concept of machine-function.

Winckelmann saw his role to be to bring the German-speaking lands up to date with France in appreciating the continuing relevance of classical literature and art, not merely to ape the forms but to create indigenous German art with classical principles as an updated guide. This would counteract what he took to be moribund Baroque forms of artistic expression, including those present in architecture.[28] The other great figure in the early German Enlightenment was the playwright, philosopher, and essayist Gottfried Lessing. Lessing's Enlightenment credentials were every bit as impeccable as Winckelmann's, but Lessing was more perceptive when it came to interpreting the classical art that was supposed to be the Polaris to the compass point of the German intellectual scene. Where Winckelmann saw semi-divine implacability, composure, and even grandeur in the most violent and distraught depictions in Greek statuary, Lessing saw (correctly, especially when applied to the Hellenistic sculptural group over which they cross swords, Laocoön) agony and willed restraint. The very art that Winckelmann was touting as the building blocks for a serene and classicized German "new art" was itself as emotion-laden as the Baroque that it was to supersede. Lessing saw that no matter how important classical ideas might be, they were a good bit more continuous with post-classical human culture than neo-classicists would admit and, therefore, should be integrated on that basis, providing a more subtle response to the Baroque than simple rejection of it.

Let's return to the analogy. The "frozen music" image is deployed with this slippery idea of a staid classical geometricity versus a moving "expressive" idea of the body in the background. Readers of Goethe, who also deploys the analogy, will fight to the end over the degree to which he is a "classicist" or a "proto-romantic." For him, the "frozen music" idea might invoke classical ideas of what the human body is, or it might presuppose a more expressionistic notion of the same, where an element of that conception would be something like a correlate to Merleau-Ponty's idea that an account of the body requires express consideration of what it is like to be a body. With Schelling, firmly entrenched in romanticism, there is little doubt that he means the second. Of course, one may come at the image from the other angle, asking what conception of music underlies the comparison. We can't go into the complexities of answering such a question here in a book on architecture, but the structure of the answer to the question will be similar to the answer from the architectural side of things. The music that was cutting edge at Goethe's time was that of Haydn, Mozart, and, as yet not fully realized, Beethoven. These composers have been grouped together under the heading of "classical" or "the classical style" on many counts, most convincingly in terms of the development of sonata form in symphonic composition.[29] If we leave out of consideration the case of Beethoven and the proclivity to read back into his earlier work the late string quartets, even the more seemingly stable cases of Haydn and

Mozart are fraught with teetering between classical and romantic sensibilities. Perhaps Haydn is the easier case: the Erdödy Quartets, op. 76 (1797), the *Seven Last Words*, op. 51 (1796), the final, so-called *London* Symphonies, nos. 93–104 (1792–5), the *Apponyi* Quartets, op. 74 (1793), and even the earlier *Paris* Symphonies, nos. 82–87 (1785–6), are quite expressionist. Mozart, often treated as the innocent *Wunderkind* whose instrumental precocity purely expressed the allegedly universal rational language of musical form, has been subject to reconsideration along lines that are not foreign to romanticism. The much-cited evidence is the musical and dramatic treatment of the title figure in the opera *Don Giovanni* (1787), but one might argue for the last of the six so-called Haydn Quartets, K. 465 (1785) as well. So, when deciphering the motto that architecture is frozen music, one must be careful to say what historical understandings of music and architecture are in play. But that does not insure that all ambiguity will be resolved.

So, where is one left? I suggest following out the idea that the analogy must be understood historically, with a bit of a twist. When one asks what form of human expression pays equal attention to the various types of musical temporality and the embodied experience of space, it seems that "dance" is almost a self-recommending reply. Much classical music at various times was concerned to conform to and reinforce popular dances of the time. Jazz, blues, rock 'n' roll, rock, and electronica also have extremely close relations to dance. Perhaps one avenue of inquiry is how architectural space relates to music that is played within it, as dance relates to music. To some, it may seem that I am just substituting a metaphor for a metaphor here. But metaphors can be more or less apt, so let's see how this one works out.

Let's revisit Frank Gehry. Consider his Walt Disney Concert Hall (2003) in downtown Los Angeles (Figure 2.8). It is not entirely fanciful or without support to describe the façade of the Concert Hall as a dance. The volumes of the façade seem like enlivened rectilinear volumes, almost as if the right-angled stuff of classical proportion had been awakened by music into rollicking movement. As are many Gehry buildings nowadays, the exterior is clad in reflective metal, intensifying the geometric dance by the reflected dance of the Los Angeles sky in the day and the city lights at night. As is the case generally with modern buildings from the time of Mies, Gropius, and Le Corbusier onward, the exterior is designed to give expression to the interior, and vice versa. The main performance space in the building, which is by all accounts a masterpiece of acoustics on a par, if not exceeding, Carnegie Hall in New York, is dominated by a multi-story free-form wood fluting incorporating into it the pipes of the main organ.

Figure 2.8 Walt Disney Concert Hall [Getty Images]

Admittedly, architecture as dance is not a very well worked out idea. The philosopher who gave the most emphasis to the dance character of music was perhaps Nietzsche. Focusing on the emergence, predominance, and then decline of tragedy as a form of ancient Greek self-understanding, he emphasizes the unity of music, dramatic movement, and narrative in Greek art. According to Nietzsche, the chorus and its function in tragedy evolved out of more primitive satyr plays, in which dance was a primary mode of expression. (The Greek word *choros* just means "dance in the round.")[30] These plays were parts of religious celebrations of the pre-Olympian god Dionysus, in which the celebrants, through intoxication and frenzied dance, both summoned the god to be present among them and threw off the experience of individuality in favor of belonging to an undifferentiated throng. Although we do not have a very precise sense of what the music that accompanied this ritual art was like, music was essential to it. Nietzsche's understanding of the meaning of music, then, is intimately bound up with its role in dance, drama, and, ultimately, the architectural places in which drama is performed.[31] This is one reason why he was initially drawn to Wagner's concept of musical drama, which posits the art work as an indivisible whole mixing music, drama, and architecture. Wagner's plans for the construction of the Bayreuth venue dedicated to the experience of his operas attest to this.

This is a complicated way to explicate the analogy laid down between architecture and music with which we started. Instead of a static idea of the pure element of architecture—disembodied space—I have substituted something like the idea of embodied experience of space in the form of dance. This allows architecture, via a more dynamic idea of formed space that underlies it, to approach in a more convincing way the condition of temporality often taken to be the inherent material of music. This frees architecture a bit from its frozenness relative to music, but it still places architecture in an inferior role, i.e., of an art form whose significance is understood in terms of another art. It is true that understanding something in terms of another thing does not necessarily mean that the thing in terms of which the understanding is reached is superior. But it is hard not to feel that this is implied, given the historical register of thinking of architecture in this way. What is perhaps most arresting about Gehry's Concert Hall is that the concept of dance as a kind of intermediary between architecture and music is given full range in the architecture without relegating the architecture to the music. Both the exterior and interior forms dance and, in doing so, complement the movement called forth in a body that listens intently to music and causes the eye and body to move in relation to the volumes and forms of the building. Gehry has achieved something quite remarkable, especially in his design of the organ gallery. Medieval churches were of course sites for the experience of much liturgical music and, fittingly, the mass of organ piping could become an important part of the overall visual experience of the church interior. Typically, registers of organ pipes maintained the linear, upwards motion in terms of which the church generally operated on the parishioner. Gehry has accepted the centrality of the organ to the hall and thus of part of this historical lineage, but has crafted the voluptuous architecture of the organ to reflect just this synthesis of music and architecture in the movement of dance. Although, as we shall discuss in Chapter 3, not all things Disney are wonderful, Gehry's Los Angeles concert hall is a stunning example of how architecture is musical and music architectural at one and the same time.

Yet another way to view music and architecture as connected to one another also involves analogies between time and space as materials of those arts. Perhaps this is even another way of interpreting the "frozen music" analogy, but the idea is in principle broader than that. Movement in music can be conceptualized physically, as above, in terms of dance. But it may also be modeled somewhat more abstractly as development. It is exceedingly difficult to give a satisfactory definition of what development in music is. This is true both because the concept "development" has been used to canvas many aspects of music and because the concept has undergone historical changes in its application. Still, for present purposes, one might venture that development is a "structural alteration in musical material, as opposed to the exposition or statement of material."[32] The "material" may be various: melodic line in chant, fugal counterpoint, or what is the most studied case, classical sonata form. The means or modalities of the alteration are also numerous: pitch, timbre, melodic counterpoint, thematic extrapolation or condensation, etc.[33] Now, if one views the material in question as essentially temporal, then development, however instantiated, is development of material in terms of its temporality. Can the space of architecture claim the same?

Some architects have thought so. Steven Holl has said that he conceives of movement through spaces in his buildings in such terms. What he has in mind is that various aspects of the passage through a series of architectural spaces correspond to the passage of one's hearing through a piece of music. So, one might rightly suggest that bodily rhythm is affected by change of perspectival line, parallax vision, the hue of color on walls, the feel of the building material, and the play of shadow and light at different times of day, in a way that is similar to the impact of melody, thematic alteration, tonality, and the "color" of instrumentation in music. Of course, there are differences, and they are telling. One cannot go backwards in hearing music. In a live setting, this is obviously impossible; but even with recorded music and modern playback capacity, one just restarts the music at a point, thereby interrupting the flow of the musical experience. When one walks through a building and one re-tracks, one is thereby creating a new path through the space, not merely "hitting rewind." If a building is complicated and subtle enough, it may call and recall responses to it that are almost infinite in number, just as Bach's *Brandenburg Concerti* might.[34]

Perhaps this is a more rewarding way to think of the relationship of music to architecture. Of course it prescinds from important matters like forms of cultural knowledge that may lie behind or within both music and architecture, and this can tempt a kind of sterile formalism on both sides of the comparison. But, if one keeps in mind that the comparison needs to be supplemented by an account of the social formation of the two arts, the more phenomenological point needn't mislead.

ARCHITECTURE IN THE ARTS: FILM

There have been many arresting renderings of architecture in film, and one might say that film has an unrivaled capacity as an artistic medium to give one a sense of being in architectural space, other than being present in the building itself. (Of course, film can also, sometimes, intentionally distort that experience, e.g., *The Cabinet of Dr. Caligari* or, more subtly, Welles' use of low angle shots in *Citizen Kane*.)

Some films not only use depictions of architecture as structural devices, but they express their filmic elements architecturally. Arguably this is the case with the opening credit shots from Hitchcock's *North by Northwest* (1959), with the famous pan down the façade of the Secretariat Building at the United Nations, its use of Grand Central Terminal in New York, or the Prairie Style mansion that is the spies' final rendezvous. Hitchcock had previously used a similar finale on the face of the Statue of Liberty in his lesser-known, but still estimable, *Saboteur* (1942). Although involving no famous landmark buildings, one might argue with good reason that *Rear Window* (1954) is the epitome of the use of architectural ideas in Hitchcock's films. Even more intensive, psychologically speaking, is the use of architecture in Michelangelo Antonioni's *Night* (*La notte*, 1960). There are many architectural forms shot in the film in a desolate aesthetic reminiscent of the sparse, metaphysical paintings of de Chirico. Antonioni's treatment of architectural elements is more inherently architectural than Hitchcock's, primarily because his use of close-ups heightens the tactile experience of the filmed buildings. But what may be most arresting is how Antonioni stultifies the temporal medium of the film at its conclusion by spatializing it in architectural terms. I am referring to the famous sequence of the vacant streets that stand in for the missed assignation of the lovers at the conclusion, a scene revisited in the stark ending of his *Eclipse* (*L'ecclise*, 1962).[35]

Up to now we have considered the relation of architecture and architectural space to the other arts in terms of conceptual hierarchies, ways in which architecture houses other arts, and analogically. Because architecture is sometimes taken to be the most "total" art, it is an interesting reversal to consider ways in which it appears *in* film. Notwithstanding very interesting accounts of film portrayal of architecture, I wish to concentrate on a more recent example—one of the opening scenes of Wim Wenders' film *Wings of Desire* (Himmel über Berlin, 1987). Unlike Tarkhovsky, who emphasizes the tactile material connection of filmed surfaces with architectural ones, or the more prevalent idea that film is, next to architecture, the best candidate for a total, immersed and, therefore, most "real" experience that art can afford, reflection on Wenders' film forces one to make another set of connections between film and architecture, having to do with the relation of space, filmic or architectural, to reflective thought generally.

Co-written with the Austrian novelist and playwright Peter Handke, the film concerns one of Handke's main preoccupations—the extent to which what seem to be transient or unremarkable experiences leave traces in history. Wenders and Handke address this theme by positing a stark contrast between two sorts of beings. On the one hand are immortal, incorporeal angels who populate the non-spatial spirit world of pre-reunified Berlin. The angels circulate among humans, attuning themselves empathically to them and entering into their thoughts. The thoughts are heard in voiced-over interior monologue. Much of this monologue explicitly involves reflection on human existential matters—the general meaning of life, difficult relationships or decisions, psychological preoccupations, etc. The angels are depicted as trench-coated, detached detectives who, although they can in some cases subtly alter the moods or thoughts of humans by attending them, cannot actively guide those whom they encounter.[36] Only children can see the angels and, although this is not made entirely clear, only those close to death can be truly assuaged by them. That is, angelic interaction with humans that can either reveal the angels or take comfort from them is only possible for those who, relatively speaking, have either just come into being as humans or are ready to succumb to their mortality. The angels' existence, as they understand it, is given over to making ephemeral thought and unobserved action permanent by entering them in a cosmic record. In this way Wenders and Handke join in the solution of the age-old problem of immortalizing, and thereby making meaningful, transient life, by imagining non-human observers, e.g., God, who take it all down and, in so doing, dignify its occurrence. Why what is transient has to be dignified at all is another question the film addresses later, but I cannot go into that here.

Philosophers divide on the question of whether all thought is expressible in language or even whether all thought is "language" in some extended sense of the word. Whatever the answer to that question might be, the film presents the humans' thoughts as uttered in an internal mental space. Perhaps Wenders could have shown thought in film pictorially, but there are many thoughts that are not imagistic in the least and, at any rate, the monologue form seems best suited for filmic portrayal of thought. As it turns out—and this is a wonderful idea that seems to have been Handke's—the angels, eternal though they are, did not learn to speak until primitive humans did so. The angels' ability to enter discrete conceptual thought seems to have grown up with the human ability to have such thought. This is entirely consistent with the angels' main function of empathy.[37]

Humans are corporeal and human thought, even if it is occasionally or even mostly internal, is situated in spatial environments subject to embodied experience. In many ways, the self-reflective sort of monologue with which Wenders invests his thinkers has a natural home in libraries. Libraries are repositories for written thought—a human record analogous to the angelic witnessing at the center of the film. The experience of reading, or perhaps an especially intensive version of it, puts in motion basic reflective capacities, and this also is part of the idea of a library as a place for thought. But, in addition to being places in which one can read, libraries are also places where one can experience a kind of stillness that is in itself conducive to reflection; they are places that provide safe harbors for letting thought find its own way, freed from the demands of hurly-burly, everyday life. These three aspects of a library that involve self-reflection—archival, lexical, and introspective—combine in myriad ways to make up a cultural background for one's embodied experience of that sort of architectural space. Of course many libraries are entirely mundane, architecturally speaking. Their architecture seems to bear scant relation to an embodied understanding of the three aspects of the human experience of libraries just listed. Some buildings, however, are sensitive precisely to this sort of experience.

In a scene of extraordinary beauty and emotional resonance, Wenders' angels attend their human charges in the Staatsbibliothek zu Berlin. The Berlin State Library, by the architects Hans Scharoun and Edgar Wisniewski, is the largest library in Germany. At the time of the making of the film, it had extra social significance as a preeminent cultural institution located at the epicenter of what was then still a divided Germany. And simply because it is located in Germany, the library is a repository of cultural memory for a culture for which concepts like "memory," "witnessing," and "forgetting" are especially pointed, to say the least. The scene, shot, as are all the opening scenes in the film, in luminous black and white, begins with a low-angle tracking shot of the ceiling of the library, which concentrates on the geometrical shapes of the light fixtures and skylights.[38] One immediately hears the murmur of a multitude of voices coursing in and out of recognition, expressive of the reading, writing, and musing thought of the humans. Both the aural and the visual point of view in the scene are in the first person, where the audience is identified with an angel (but not, strikingly, with any of the characters in the film who are angelic). The angels tap into this experiential ocean as one would, were one attempting to listen discreetly to a conversation at a party, by concentrating and filtering out the rest. This concentration is shown in the film by the angels closing their eyes or by touching the mortals. The action of shutting the eyes (their ears cannot shut in this way), allows for ambiguity. This may be a sign of concentration or, as is sometimes the case, a kind of attempted retreat or even a wincing in pain at the overwhelming number of thoughts calling out for angelic recognition or at the sometimes painful content of a particular thought. Or, closing the eyes might express an attitude of allowing the thought to wash over one. All are suggested.

Among the thoughts present that are individually discernable are ones about the exiled German-Jewish intellectual Walter Benjamin (whose Berlin Childhood, Circa 1900 is a rumination on a "lost Berlin" very much in keeping with Wenders' concerns), ones by a young Turkish mother, and a passage read in Hebrew from the Torah. The thoughts of the dispossessed are of special importance and this fact is brought home by the introduction of a Homeric, "storyteller" (Erzähler) figure, an elderly Jewish man who has returned to Berlin only to find the Berlin of his youth effaced (in particular, he searches in vain for the old Potsdamerplatz). We are introduced to him as he laboriously climbs the central stair leading from the large ground floor atrium of the library to the first level of open stacks. His thoughts are turned to the role of humans themselves in preserving what might otherwise be erased—a theme of particular importance for a German Jew or any Jew, for that matter. He is, in essence, the human counterpart to the angels. They record the transient in the record book of eternity, all the time longing for the immediacy of corporeal experience; the storyteller is human, is concerned that the possibility of even the best human efforts at preserving a record of the past are ineffectual, and, for that reason, yearns for a measure of stability, a share of eternity. To make things more complex, Peter Falk, playing himself, is a fallen angel—one who has, by dint of sheer will, passed over from immortality to mortality. He completes the dialectical triangle, with the storyteller and the angels describing the other internal angles, by representing the trading in of eternal watchfulness, or its mortal near-equivalent, for the pleasures of transience. In a later scene in the film, Falk is at an *Imbiß* when he senses an angel nearby and proceeds to describe to him the simple goodness of a cigarette (bad example!) or of rubbing one's hands together to ward off the cold.[39]

Let's return to the Staatsbibliothek. The storyteller reaches the landing of the stair and rests in a chair, readying himself for the business of reading and writing by putting on his glasses. This is the same chair in which the angel Damiel (who will later cross over, as did Falk) is seen previously to close his eyes in order to distance himself from the ever-present human thought flooding the building. Wenders means us to compare the two sitters, one yearning for infinity and the other for its opposite. For the one, thought is potentially ephemeral and insubstantial in the face of time; for the other, thought is what is most forceful and omnipresent, approaching in the eternal realm the very substantiality it lacks in the profane.[40]

In addition to the rising and falling tide of voices, the

library scene is accompanied by a non-deictic, purely vocalized choir reminiscent of the "Sirènes" section of Debussy's *Nocturnes*.[41] I have been using sea imagery in describing some of the effects and events in this sequence, and it is with that and the mention of the choral element in this part of the film that I would like to turn more specifically to the question of how the film incorporates architectural space into its filmic treatment of the imbrication of memory and forgetting. The library stacks open out to a large multi-storey atrium by means of balconied overlooks. There are several wide-angle panning shots that involve one in the sense of immense openness of the structure. The angels use the balconies as perches, sitting or standing on or by them. This gives the atrium the aspect of an airie, but one might also think of it as a depth, the depth of an ocean, by which mariner-angels stand, surveying the thought-filled void and one another on its shores. Whether one takes to heart the aquatic imagery or the avian, the point remains that the atrium is the architectural center of the building and of the filming of it, and not just because of the power of the filmed image. It is so because of the thematic relevance of the architectural void as the dimension that both presents the utter isolation of the thoughts of humans from one another and the distance between bloodless angels and their full-blooded charges. Sirens are supernatural creatures who ply their deadly trade by the sea, most famously in Book XII of the *Odyssey*. They prey on sailors' wanderlust and homesickness in order to tempt them to a watery ruin. They are:

[T]hose creatures who spellbind any man alive, whoever comes their way. Whoever draws too close, off guard, and catches the Sirens' voices in the air—no sailing home for him,

no wife rising to meet him, no happy children beaming up
at their father's face. The high, thrilling song of the Sirens
will transfix him, lolling there in their meadow, round them
heaps of corpses, rotting away, rages of skin shriveling on
their bones . . .

(ll. 45–52)[42]

Yearning from both sides of the immortal/mortal divide is
at the heart of Wenders' film. The divide is the dimension
within which the interaction of the angelic and the human
occurs and is described as architectural space within the film.
The alteration between the distance and proximity of the two
realms is realized by this filmic depiction of space in which
bodies and thought move in parallel yet without unity.

Three

Buildings don't exist in vacuums. They are surrounded by other buildings in urban or suburban contexts and by nature in rural ones. When an architect builds she does so on a site amidst other preexisting things. It is common to hear architects speak about the "site specificity" of their projects. This idea, borrowed from its more familiar context in large-scale sculpture, captures two directions of fit between a given building and its surroundings, be they buildings or nature. On the one hand—and this is by far the most common way to think of the force of the idea of site-specific art—a project is supposed to be sensitive to existing, or perhaps even potentially existing, elements that surround it. Wright's Falling Water is often cited as an example of a structure that so blends in with the landscape around it that it becomes an integral, non-invasive part of its surroundings. Lots of ways, and degrees, of such fitting in are possible for architecture, some of which we shall discuss in this chapter. Imagine an architect touting her next big project by emphasizing how essentially dissimilar it will be and how it will not fit in, and it becomes readily apparent how much normative force the idea of fit enjoys.[1] On the other hand, "site-specific" can refer to how the *site* is reorganized in terms of the building. Buildings are not passive guests in their given surroundings: they place demands on what surrounds them and, ultimately, create new surroundings in virtue of their presence. Both of these directions of fit—buildings fitting into their surroundings and surroundings being fit for their buildings—are present in any architectural event.

Even though this bidirectional fit is always at issue, there are cases in which this is pointedly so. There are cases where projects make it a main part of the content of the architectural experience of a building that it should include an experience of its fittingness. And there are cases where given surroundings are, for a variety of reasons experiential and political, very sensitive to change. In what follows we shall look at issues involving one particular category of site specificity: the urban context, where buildings are playing off one another. As was the case with the first two chapters, a phenomenological chord is struck in the discussion, but it sometimes gives way to more recognizably ethical and social-political themes relevant to urban studies. As it will turn out, the link between phenomenology of architecture and an ethics of architecture is not incidental, although phenomenology does stress quite a different dimension of an ethical response to architecture from that which is often considered. One way to put the connection—which will have to be provisional until we discuss it in earnest later—is to say that phenomenology of architecture turns out to be *anti-formalist* in a way that highlights the ethical paucity of some ways of thinking about the meaning of buildings. Its anti-formalism also casts some recent attempts at revitalizing architecture with "an ethics" as formalist in spite of themselves.

THE NELSON-ATKINS MUSEUM REDUX

Let's return to the Bloch Addition to the Nelson-Atkins Museum in Kansas City. One of the main issues with the

Addition was situating it appropriately in relation to the pre-existing Beaux Arts museum building and its ample grounds. The museum fronts the street with an expansive, sloping, mall-like lawn that provides vistas up to the impressive façade of the old museum building. This plan was intended, no doubt, to frame the building rather classically and would not at all have looked out of place in Washington, D.C. where numerous malls are deployed to this effect. This is a strong statement of civic pride and grandeur, and one does not tread heavily on such a plan.

It was fortunate for the architect, Steven Holl, that the classicizing ground plan had already been subject to some artistic intervention. Scattered across the front and rear lawns are monument-sized sculptures of upended shuttlecocks courtesy of the artists Claes Oldenburg and Coosje van Bruggen. Installed in 1994, Oldenburg and van Bruggen's *Shuttlecocks* are conceived to be the remnants of a giant game of badminton played on the lawn, with the stately museum building serving conceptually as a net. Taking the rather explicit sense of embodied civic pride in classical form as a spur to their playful piece, Oldenburg and van Bruggen gently send up the museum's classical bearing. *Shuttlecocks* makes the museum as it existed an element of the artwork, but not in a way that effaces the cultural heritage of the building or its grounds. It is, all told, an extremely successful piece of site-specific art that allows the fit between it and the site to run in both directions at once.

In this way *Shuttlecocks* loosens up the site that Holl had to deal with as his given and, because it is a work of pop or conceptual art, it does so in a way that will not be directly in competition with Holl's more phenomenological method of dealing with what he is given as surroundings. Still, the proposals entered into competition for the commission show that all the architects save Holl proposed adding onto the back of the existing museum structure, the main building still asserting its classical authority. Holl's responsiveness to the site has become as admired as is the internal space of the Addition. He chose to align the Addition stage left of the existing structure, embedding the new building in hillocks that gracefully descend on a slope similar in grade to the formal front lawn.[2] The new structure is visible as what Holl calls "lenses" that both complement the posture of the existing Beaux Art museum in their geometric purity and extend the design of the overall site. A very extensive and important sculpture garden is, in part, located on the grassed-in roof spaces of the terraced lenses, linked by a winding path that utilizes subtle compound angles of ascent and descent to give the walker a feeling of "extended balance" similar to the experience one has in some of the interior spaces of the museum. Holl's approach is holistic. Not only are the old and new building complementary; the site is extended and held together by the buildings in a way that is perhaps even stronger than the preexisting classical grid imposed by the main building alone. Moreover, the sense in which one is inside the Addition or outside it is made thematically and experientially complex in two ways. The landscape is included in the interior by way of the Addition's fenestration. Likewise, the inside is brought outside by means of the intimate role the lenses play in structuring the sculpture garden.

The reciprocal site specificity of the Bloch Addition is further enhanced by the treatment given to the parking garage. The Nelson-Atkins Museum is located in a city that, for many, will be visited by automobile. Prior to the Bloch Addition, parking was scarce and located above ground directly behind the main building. So dead was this space that, as I just mentioned, all projects entered in competition for the Addition assumed that this would be the location of the new structure. Holl's entry envisioned this space to be left open for a major work of site-specific sculpture. Parking was moved below ground but not with the usual dismal results. The space taken up with the above-ground parking is now occupied by a major work by the sculptor Walter De Maria, *One Sun/34 Moons*. This work consists in a rectangular reflecting pond which has embedded in its bottom several circular glass lenses that receive light at night from the underground parking garage and transmit daylight to the garage. The idea of a reflecting pond is of course entirely in keeping with the classical mall-like site of the original museum. Translating light to and from the garage brings that area aesthetically and architecturally directly into the site. And the luminescence of the disks ties together with Holl's glassed lenses, both receivers and dispersers of light. In a way reminiscent of the 1950s' and 1960s' concern for architectural and artistic expression in the Age of Travel, Holl's plan makes what is often treated as a merely pragmatic demand to be tolerated—the need for car parking—into a part of the overall experience of the museum complex.

Contrast Holl's treatment of the site in Kansas City with I.M. Pei's solution for an underground entrance into the Louvre (Figure 3.1). However one ultimately feels about the overall merit of Pei's steel-reinforced glass pyramid, three things must be allowed. First, it is an architectural structure the judgment of which is intimately bound up with how it fits the site (and how the site fits it). Its début in 1989 occasioned extraordinarily hostile reaction from the general population; the reaction among architects was more temperate.

Figure 3.1 Pyramid, Louvre [Keith Levit]

The Louvre is of course a building and grounds of immense cultural significance for France and beyond. Pei's assertion was just that—a blatantly modern structure that took its root in an archetypical historical context. Second, modern though it is—much in keeping with all of Mitterrand's *grands projets*—the pyramid offered its sacrifice to the gods of tradition in the form of its, well, form. It is a glass pyramid, after all, geometrically if not exactly classically proportioned and, thus, transparent to the architectural will of the Sun King. It is not as if someone gave the space over to Robert Venturi's dream of Las Vegas as eye-candy! So, the pyramid does not entirely ignore at least some of the architectural principles that guided the building of the initial palace—although, of course, it did distill those principles in what some may think an unacceptably abstract way. Third, and most to the point here, if judged merely in terms of how well it answers to the site in terms of fitting into it, Pei's building is palpably less successful than Holl's.

Of course, "fitting in," even in the extended sense that involves transforming a site in terms of new building, may not be the point of Pei's pyramid. The grand gesture is a fixation in Paris, to be encountered everywhere from a philosophy seminar to one's favorite bistro. In the U.S. and Canada it is less present, so ill-fated works like Richard Serra's *Tilted Arc* and Daniel Libeskind's aggressive extension to the Royal Ontario Museum in Toronto are perhaps less well tolerated. *Tilted Arc*, which used to bisect Federal Plaza in New York City, was famously removed over the artist's (litigated) objection when people complained about it.[3] Libeskind's extension, which opened in 2007, is a glass and metal-clad, crystal-like outgrowth protruding from a corner of the museum building. It utterly dominates the curb-look of the building. The original Toronto museum building was pretty undistinguished, and there was not much to say for the plaza between the two towers either. In such cases architecture might be said to operate with a freer hand, since there are fewer inherent demands imposed on the site by existing buildings of merit. Additionally, insensitivity to site might be either merely apparent or something that one wants. Take Libeskind as an example. The Toronto extension is inspired by an estimable collection of natural crystal formations in the museum. Libeskind's Jewish Museum in Berlin needs to rearrange its environs in terms of it—that is one thing the absence of Jewish culture in Berlin after the Holocaust might require. Insensitivity to surroundings may be, in some instances, the sensitive response to them.

MORE IS MORE

Mies van der Rohe famously said (or didn't) that "less is more." By this he meant the fewer inessential, non-structural elements to a building the better. One of Mies' most stunning achievements along these lines is the campus of the Illinois Institute for Technology, located on the eastside of Chicago. It is not very often that an architect gets to build an entire campus full of buildings—to work, as painters used to say, on such a broad canvas. A campus is, at least ideally, a highly integrated, fairly total environment for living a life of the mind. Academic teaching, learning, and research take place in such places, as do lives informed by such purposes. As we shall see a bit later in this chapter, the idea of building a "total environment" has been intoxicating for some modern architects. Mies, more than many of his other illustrious modernist colleagues, got a chance to do just that.

It is said that when it was decided that air conditioning was something in the order of a necessity for the campus, Mies was put out by the way the condenser units appeared like warts on all his carefully formed buildings. One can only imagine what his reaction would have been when it was decided, many years later, that a new train station for the campus was needed. Any new building proximal to Mies' buildings would of necessity make a great difference to the overall architectural character of the campus, so the train station would be an issue no matter who built it. In 2003 the architect Rem Koolhaas completed the McCormick-Tribune Campus Center at IIT, which incorporates the railway station with a 10,000 square foot (930 square meter) student center.

This raises the stakes, in a way, on the discussion of the preceding section. It is one thing to build with sensitivity to what one takes a site to need and attempt to establish an equilibrium between site and building. But most sites will not have famous architecture already on them. The Beaux Arts of the pre-existing Nelson Atkins Museum is attractive, but not sacrosanct. The Louvre may be sacrosanct but, one might argue, this is due mostly to its place in history and not to its sheer architectural merit. The IIT Campus is unlike either of these two examples. Here one builds adjacent to an icon of architectural high modernism—never mind the historical point that Mies was the architectural director of studies at IIT and conceived it as the successor to the defunct Bauhaus. The issue becomes: what does architectural site specificity mean when the site is already specified by great architecture?

Can site specificity be, so to speak, cumulative? That is, can a once specified site be specified over again? A simple answer may seem obvious. So long as the new project respects the site specificity of the first in its own specification of site, then the case is no more difficult than any other. The existing building is just a new element that has to be brought into the picture. This may introduce complications in specific cases, but there is nothing generally problematic about the case. On the face of it, this line of reasoning seems perfectly right, but what it does not sufficiently take into account is the sometimes extreme specification levied on a site by iconic architecture. To put the point somewhat hyperbolically: truly great buildings tend to go beyond site specificity; they are almost site *determining*. That is, their presence seeks to close down the possibility for other building or, at least, the possibility for other strong building. Whatever comes later will, at best, occupy the back seat.

Many judge that Koolhaas' McCormick-Tribune Center successfully negotiates the difficult terrain of building an important building on a site that is dominated by important buildings. Koolhaas is a master of this sort of thing: he characteristically builds in thick urban contexts in which attention to this set of concerns is a must. Intervention in the IIT campus—a place that Mies cultivated as his own total architectural

environment—is perhaps the high water mark of Koolhaas'
practice in this regard. (The McCormick-Tribune complex is
startlingly apt as an Information Age transit center and ranks,
with the Seattle Library, as one of Koolhaas' most important
buildings.) How does it work? This is a complex question that
would require a book in its own right, but a few things are
worth mentioning. First, Koolhaas doesn't compete. There
is nothing formally Mies-like about the architecture of the
McCormick-Tribune Center: it is decidedly not a piece of
Platonic architecture and its focal point, the rail station, is the
polar opposite of that aesthetic. It also does not compete by
being so different from Mies' buildings that one might see the
new buildings as usurpers. The primary orientation toward
the rail station helps here—a fairly discrete use, somewhat at a
distance from the iconic instructional architecture. Second,
time is also on Koolhaas' side: while presumably no one
would want to downplay Mies' continued architectural legacy
on the IIT campus, his presence as an educator in his own
vision of architectural modernism is past. The meaning of
Mies' buildings there has gone from a normative one of "this
is how to build," or even "this is how to live," to a consciousness of the role of the campus in the history of modern
architecture. The idea, still normative, that replaces Mies' own
prescriptions is that of great modernist architecture, and that
is something that Koolhaas can operate with and within.
Whether one sees Koolhaas as a modernist himself or as a
post-modernist using the concept of great modern architecture as a semiotic springboard doesn't much matter. The
point is that the McCormick Tribune buildings extend the
presence of modernist architecture on the campus, and it is
this *idea* that unites the newly formed site-complex. In essence,
the new architecture draws a line from the era of Mies' great

activity and influence through the great period of Jet Age urban architecture of speedy arrivals and departures up to the present. And that is something for which IIT, positioned as it is as a centerpiece in that tradition, can be grateful.

MASS BUILDING: SEEING AND BEING SEEN

Nowadays in the United States most building projects are realized in the sprawling suburbs that eke out from the major metropolitan areas: New York, Los Angeles, and Chicago to be sure, but also Houston, Las Vegas, and Seattle. Although there are exceptions—one thinks especially of Frank Lloyd Wright and Richard Neutra here, but there are others—it has not been the case that signature architectural projects have claimed America's suburban imagination. The city is still where the action is, and it is easy to see why. Cities are still the power centers of business, government, and culture for most of the country. Many people choose to move out of cities for domestic reasons, but capital, both actual and cultural, concentrates itself in the cities.

This is an old story, as is the story of making, unmaking, and remaking architecture in the urban context. Among other things, cities provide the architect with an idea of a total built environment. In Chapter 1 we considered ways that buildings are experienced phenomenologically. We saw that some architects expressly incorporate phenomenological ideas in their building practices, so as to enrich our experience of body, building, and their interrelation. To be enriched seems like an altogether good thing. But another way to put the point is less salutary: architects (and not just phenomenologically based ones) tend to want to prescribe responses to their buildings and intend that their buildings act on people in prescribed ways. The word "control" may seem too strong to describe these aims, unless, one turns from individual buildings or small clusters of them to putting one's mark on a large swathe of urban real estate. The idea of remaking large amounts of urban living space in accordance with any one among many overarching ideas of how people *should* live has been an extremely tempting one for architects and urban planners alike.

Take a famous historical case. Recently I was walking back from the Left Bank when I passed the main entrance to the Sorbonne, the oldest of the now many divisions of the University of Paris system. The University of Paris was for a good period of time the center of European intellectual life. The university was founded in 1215, pre-dating the universities at Oxford and Cambridge by the better part of a century, and all but monopolized the study and teaching of theology and philosophy, the preeminent medieval intellectual disciplines, until the rise of late medieval empirical science that finally shifted the center of influence to England. This historical heritage is reflected in the Sorbonne's immediate surroundings. Although the central buildings of the university are not medieval in the least, the narrow plaza facing the university can give some idea of how insular medieval street arrangements might have been. In point of fact, it is but a faint reminder: medieval streets tended to be extraordinarily narrow— alleyways really—being constituted by whatever space was left over after property owners had built their buildings out to the limits of their parcels. Streets were, in many cases, the detritus of well-exercised property management, the outer walls of buildings forming, on either side, the defining inner walls of the street. The plaza outside the entrance to the Sorbonne is much roomier than that, but the point is that it is extremely closed-in by modern standards, able to support an array of intimate cafés and isolated enough for a street party or two.

Or, a barricade or two. Given a little historical knowledge, what springs to mind when one passes through the square is how easy it would be to defend the area. Hausmann's *grands boulevards* may have been tailored to allow for freer troop movements into areas of unrest and to thwart latter-days communards (to be fair, they also improved sanitation, never before a Parisian mainstay), but the Sorbonne was spared this.[4] The hilly geography was probably enough, but one gets the sense that, so long as it was *only* college students protesting, that could be tolerated. Of course, the boulevards did not stop protests—the demonstrations of May 1968 took place for the most part in such streets—but it *is* easier to fire tear-gas into crowds in such a venue.

Hausmann's thoroughfares cut through extensive networks of twisting streets. As epochal as this was for nineteenth-century Paris, such urban spring cleaning was not unprecedented. Sixtus V did much the same for Rome, with the intent of improving ingress and egress to and from the most popular Christian shrines in the city. Nor was the lesson lost on posterity. Robert Moses, the titan of city planning in post-World War II New York, caused super-highways to run over and through many traditional New York neighborhoods, dismembering them irrevocably (it was also on his watch that many high-rise public housing projects, now virtually synonymous with deprivation and crime, were realized). Even in New York, Moses was not an entirely new phenomenon: the financial district, Central Park, etc. were all urban projects realized by displacing poor tenants and squatters.

Life will out—it will form and reform itself even around what might have first seemed like insurmountable obstacles and often in unpredictable ways. That is to say that even the most disruptive incursions into a deeply seated and unified form of architectural life will end in another form of architectural living around which may grow an increasing potential for reunification along quite different lines from those planned. Might not heterogeneity of architecture promote value as well? It has recently been argued—by architects as diverse as Robert Venturi and Bernard Tschumi—that this is the case.[5] This theme may be modulated into the phenomenological register. Perhaps many varied architectural experiences, some radically disjunctive with one another, will open out new possibilities for embodied experience of spatial surroundings than would otherwise be provided by even very rich homogeneity. Two competing models might emerge. Granting for the sake of argument that becoming aware of new experiential possibilities (and actualizing some of them) is generally desirable, one can favor either total holistic architectural environments that expand one's experience *intensively*, i.e., by drawing one deeper and deeper into the given environment.[6] Or one might think that an array of different experiences, perhaps even ones that require shock effects of passing between radically different sorts of architectural experience, expand one's horizons *extensively*. The more types one experiences (and the more one experiences their disjunction) the more one experiences, full stop.

TOTAL URBANISM

Either way, the idea that a city is a way to realize the deep experiential potential of architecture is popular. In the twentieth century this idea that the best and most transformative architectural effects can occur through the total planning of large urban areas was intractably linked to the phenomenon of urban utopianism. Branching out from a center concept of control of lived responses to single buildings, several influential architects articulated visions of how that control could be intensified by extending it to groups of buildings and, finally, to whole cities. "Utopia" means "no-place," but can also exploit a near-homonym in its original ancient Greek source to connote a "good place." Put them together and you have a serviceable gloss of the concept of utopia: a purportedly good place that is no place. More particularly it is a no place *because* it is conceived to be such a good place. The vehicle for realizing these places was invariably architectural control and, for this reason, many came to see these visions as totalitarian—perhaps even as of a piece with other totalitarian impulses present in the twentieth century.

Let's begin with the dreamers. Le Corbusier and Wright, to name just the most prominent exponents of utopian architecture in the twentieth century, entertained grandiose schemes for reforming humanity along modern lines through massive architectural change. Le Corbusier's atelier and the various incarnations of Wright's studio both placed enormous emphasis on the "totality" of individual buildings. These architects were themselves artisans and had built fixtures and furnishings that were not only compatible with their architecture but were considered by them to be integral parts of it. The Bauhaus started out as a place where architects were trained across the crafts, as did Wright's Taliesin studio. Le Corbusier is perhaps better known to the general public for his chair design than his buildings. One can also assert this about Mies—who has not sat in a Barcelona chair? Given this extraordinary attention to the detail and coherence of single habitats, it is perhaps not surprising that these architects were involved with urban design. After all, the carefully engineered environment of the single building (a "machine for life" was Le Corbusier's unlovely phrase for it) could be all but spoiled simply by stepping outside. "Outside" was the enemy, for there you were confronted with the contingent, unplanned and undisciplined riot of soul-stultifying "mere buildings" (not to mention swimming pools, suburban lawns, vacant lots, old factories, etc.)

The phrase "total architecture" originates with Walter Gropius,[7] but it was Le Corbusier and Wright who each put the idea to paper. Le Corbusier's most famous proposal to build a total architectural environment is his 1925 Plan Voisin for Paris (Figure 3.2). According to the plan, the Marais was to be leveled without trace and in its place were to be erected cruciform towers on a Cartesian grid. In one grand swipe of the hand, what was the medieval market at the heart of the city, as well as the primary neighborhood of Parisian Jews,

Figure 3.2 Plan Voisin, Le Corbusier and Jeanneret [Architectural Publishers Artemis]

would be gone. (Le Corbusier was an anti-Semite and a Vichy functionary during World War II.) Streets were arranged only for automotive use; the network of pedestrian passages and alleys were to be abolished. The tower complexes were surrounded by open parkland. The entire perceptual effect of the proposal was, it seems, best appreciated from an airplane. In fact, the Plan Voisin is a more specific proposal of a general urban plan that Le Corbusier had set forth three years earlier called "La Ville Contemporaine." It was designed for three million inhabitants and would require roughly the land mass of Los Angeles. Its plan was typically linear, clear-cut and upward: miles and miles of grids of residential housing in towers of ten storeys, with a business center of twenty-four sixty-storey towers. The business section and some of the internal quadrants consisting of the residential towers were bounded by streets, but some of the outer regions of the residential space were laid out on continuous park space, presaging the idea of an "open" city where life was lived in the clouds overlooking a verdant carpet below.

The Plan Voisin was never built of course, but this did not stop Le Corbusier from dreaming. La Ville Radieuse (1931) extends his idea of the open city. The main difference in the plan from the earlier conceptions of a grid-bound city of high rises was not the grid, nor the high rises—both are present in abundance. It was rather a move away from the idea of a central point around which the city was to be organized. Le Corbusier's earlier urbanism carried with it the idea that the more central to the plan the buildings were, the denser and higher they were plotted. This, in turn, reflects an acceptance on his part of a division in the city between business and leisure and perhaps a further one between the more urban upper classes and the less urban middle and working classes.

Ville Radieuse distributes the towers evenly across the park base. All access roads are above ground and all main thoroughfares are outside the city proper. Roof gardens (*jardins suspendus*), deployed in several of Le Corbusier's domestic projects, most famously in the iconic Villa Savoye (1931), figure prominently in realizing the stated aim of the plan: to afford those living in the city unparalleled experience of light, open space, and nature. This merely conceptual master plan was specified further into two proposals for building in Rio de Janeiro and Algiers. Kenneth Frampton points out that these unbuilt proposals show a developing side to Le Corbusier's urbanism that embraces more expressionistic elements, e.g., the switch from X-shaped towers to Y-shaped ones, the tapering of the main structures to the elliptical shoreline in the harbors for which they were intended, etc.[8] On a smaller scale, this de-rationalization can be seen in some of the architect's later projects, most notably the stunning Chapel Ronchamp (1955).

Wright's vision for what he termed "Usonion" (a fore-shortening of "United States of North America") life shares many features with Le Corbusier's urbanism but also diverges from it in several respects.[9] Unlike Wright's Prairie Style works, some of which were very labor-intensive and costly, Usionian architecture was designed to be moderately priced within the reach of, if not the Average Joe, the upwardly mobile executive. (Wright projected the houses as costing on average $5,000 in 1935 but more advanced examples ranged from to $60,000 to $75,000.) While not Prefab in the sense usually associated with modern architectural movements— Wright was too much an organicist for that—the projects were more uniform than Wright's previous domestic architecture. This is especially true of a limited run of later Usonian designs that used readymade concrete blocks and which are sometimes called "Usonian Automatic." South Bend, Indiana, where I live, boasts two Wright houses, one that is two doors down the street from my own house and in the Prairie Style (the DeRhodes House, 1906) and a Usonian house (the Mossberg House, 1948). The Mossberg House is the better of the two. It shows how wonderfully unified and rich the Wright aesthetic can remain in Usonian work. Wright continued to build very expensive custom houses after the Usonian turn in his practice, but it is Usonianism that is at the heart of his urbanism.

What exactly does the term "Usonian" mean? It is hard to say. Wright associated it with his inchoate ideas on social democratic reform. Wright began producing these houses in the Depression era (the Jacobs House of 1936 is generally agreed to be the first Usonian building) and saw the houses as responses to the economic issues of the day on the order of an architectural New Deal. His great foray into urban planning, his never-built proposal for Broadacre City (1935), was based on the federal land grant program that would allot one-acre building sites per citizen. This availability—strikingly similar to the land rights secured for settlers by the Northwest Ordinance of 1785 for the geographical region that now boasts the densest accumulation of Wright projects—would allow for an exodus from the distraught cities and what was their Mammon according to Wright—rent. Wright's cities, if one can call them that, were "all over" affairs. They were to be decentralized park-like communities in which the distinction between urban and rural use no longer applied. Unlike Le Corbusier's utopian *villes* Broadacre City did not eschew automobiles, it coveted them. Each Usonian home was fitted with a carport (some were designated "five-car houses"!) and, as environmentally friendly as Wright's houses were intended by him to be, he was ever eager to assert the right to drive and burn up as much gasoline as one cared to. Wright's vision was specifically anti-urban in many senses, but it was not truly suburban. In fact, Wright never would have used the term "suburban" in our sense to describe any of his planning. His chief intent was to erase the skyscraper downtowns around which suburbs huddled. Without the urban, in the old sense, there could not be a suburban. Nonetheless, the land-use plan that undergirds Broadacre City is an unwitting precursor to the contemporary wave of buying up small farms and turning them into track housing. To be sure, Wright intended Broadacre to be a Jeffersonian-inspired critical counter-project to be set over and against mainline urban planning, including the planning of exurbs and suburbs. It is ironic, and perhaps even tragic, that many of its elements were able to be absorbed by the status quo.

The sociologist Richard Sennett points out that much of the impulse driving Le Corbusier in his urbanism was to efface the age of Paris—i.e., the worn surface of the existing buildings of the Marais, and what was (by Le Corbusier's lights) its hodgepodge of structures, both of which attest to its history. History must be destroyed as a precondition to spatial creation. Thus, Sennett writes that Le Corbusier's motivation is to "destroy the differences which have accumulated in space for the sake of affirming this difference in time."[10] That seems right. The idea that one would just plow under the Marais to make way for *anything* is astonishing; the idea that one would do so as a precondition for realizing architectural Nirvana does seem an exercise in temporal dislocation. It is not merely an act of severe temporal distancing; it is, rather, one of stepping outside of time altogether, which is, after all, what Nirvana is about. Sennett's point is not just that Le Corbusier's plans, were they accepted, would have resulted in an inability to appreciate the historical nature of the site. Presumably, the contemporary city would have aged as well and in time allowed for a truncated version of the experience of historical time. But it is important not to be too abstract here. What is being replaced is primarily a way of life—a form of community—and, with it, a certain ethical continuity.[11] Wright comes out somewhat better in this regard. While Broadacre City would have transformed farmland every bit as much as Le Corbusier's plan for the Marais was to efface the city, unlike Le Corbusier, Wright was more responsive to what were then taken to be the realities of modern life—e.g., the importance of the automobile, the need for mixed-use integration in communities, etc. Of course Wright's proposal was still weighted down with Jazz Age zaniness and plain old Midwest hokum: ideas like drive-in churches, personal helicopters (what he termed "aerotors"), and money that would lose face-value over time, thereby encouraging spending (money is time!).

As these two examples make clear, architect-led urban utopianism is not a pretty sight. Even if it is the case that total buildings are desirable, this does not imply that total cities or suburbs are. What tends to get lost is that, no matter how controlling one thinks single buildings should or should not be, cities involve community and communities can't and shouldn't be legislated into existence. Communities emerge from disparate and contingent circumstances and make up what general form of life sustains them from such particular materials.

COMMUNITY LIFE

To be in a community is to belong to it. It is to live within a structure of ways of treating others as members of the community in question and ways of valuing and evaluating others who are not. That is not to say, of course, that one can't orient oneself meaningfully in a foreign community. I can visit the Faroe Islands, recognize that there is a self-sustaining community among the fishermen there, perhaps even come to understand a great deal about that community, and still fail to be a part of it. Understanding a community at least in part in terms of its power to instill and maintain a sense of belonging to it raises the question of whether and in what sense there are constraints on collections of people constituting a community. When one approaches the question in the terms we are considering—i.e., in terms of urban planning and its relation to architecture and architectural space—attention naturally turns to questions of the size of the community, its geographical locale, and the expression of its sense of belonging in terms of its buildings. Are the buildings "indigenous"? What might that mean—i.e., does it mean made of indigenous materials, made by local artisans in a style well-known as that of the locale in question? Or does "indigenous" refer as well to the self-conception of the people and whether the architecture and urban plan reflects this?

There is great disagreement about how big such a community can be and still retain a powerful enough ethical hold on one—Rousseau seemed to think no bigger than his adopted hometown Geneva, other theorists tend to even smaller groupings—but one component of such group adhesiveness is very likely to be bodily proximity of the inhabitants going about their daily lives. But one needn't be a Luddite and embrace a return to some specious notion of "the land," leaving behind the cities and their environs. The point that community requires closeness is much more general and is readily applicable to human populations that are recognizably urban and will stay that way. The architectural and urban historian Lewis Mumford advocated return to something like a medieval town model that promoted intimacy, pedestrian traffic, and multi-use neighborhoods—just what Le Corbusier and Wright hated.[12] For him the more idealizing proponents of the City of Tomorrow would have been the New Romans founding imperial centers, towards which "all roads run," as the saying goes, and whose rationales were connected to the acquisition and display of imperial spoils.[13] Jane Jacobs criticized what she took to be the twin evils that imperil the vitality of urban environments: suburban flight and skyscraper projects of those like Le Corbusier. Both Le Corbusier and Wright are for her representatives of the decentralizing of the city that stems originally from the English Garden City movement.[14] She lays at the Frenchman's doorstep the ills of the New York City Projects, built on the model of the "radiant city."[15] But she also faults Wright and Mumford for reliance on Jeffersonian agrarian ideals that anchored the Garden City movement as well. Her *The Death and Life of Great American Cities* has been the single most influential book on urban planning of the last half-century. For Jacobs, modern urbanism tends towards a division of uses, isolates what should be intertwining dimensions of human life and, as we saw with Le Corbusier's proposal for the Marais, severs urban locales from the history in terms of which they have developed and make sense. Jacobs lived for much of her life in Greenwich Village and took it to be an excellent indication of what urban mixed-use complexity engenders. Industrial, commercial, and residential life is present throughout the Village (this is still true, except for the industrial part) and this gives a sense of belonging to the community along many dimensions at once—what she labels "diversity." For every Le Corbusier

On Architecture

who disregards the numbing effect of uniformity of the great projects within the city center, there is for Jacobs a "decentrist" who errs at the opposite extreme by advocating suburban spread. Set-backs, parkland and green space are not cure-alls for her and, by themselves, secure very little in the way of ethically and socially responsible planning.

Jacobs is a kind of Socrates of urban planning, writing from outside the academy, in which pointless in-fighting can be all-consuming. Her banner has been flown by a number of hands in the service of many causes. In the wake of critiques like hers, architects working in the modernist tradition have more or less abandoned grand planning on the scale of a Le Corbusier or Wright. The whole idea of site specificity that we discussed earlier and the correlative idea that a building has to be appropriate to its surroundings have reentered urban planning theory with a vengeance. Who would dare think of plopping a high-rise project in the Marais now! But, as responsive as urban planning has become to issues raised by Jacobs and others, there are some surprisingly forced allegiances with her work that are uncritically accepted.

THE NEW URBANISM

What I have in mind here is the so-called New Urbanism movement. It would be wrong to think that this movement is homogenous. There are many types of appeal to go back to the village and the role of architecture within it. There is hardly one idea of what sort of village one might go back to, in the first place, and, in the second, there is no single way back that has claimed univocal support. Roughly speaking, however, there are two main architecture types that have been proposed as proper to the newly urban.

One of these has roots in Vitruvian principles and is recognizably neo-classical. I happen to teach at a college, the University of Notre Dame, whose school of architecture is deeply committed to this way of teaching its subject matter. For all the ink spilt in propounding neo-classicism as a vehicle for rediscovering urban communal life, it has not won as many adherents in New Urbanism as has a return to vernacular late nineteenth- and early twentieth-century small town architecture. It is in this style, with principles of planning reminiscent of early suburbanism, that the two most extensive New Urbanist towns have been built: Seaside, the first vernacular New Urbanist community, outside Panama City, Florida; and Celebration, owned and operated by the Disney Corporation and located in Oseola County, Florida on the outskirts of Orlando. In what may turn out to be the most important book in architectural planning since Jacobs, *Suburban Nation: The Rise and the Decline of the American Dream*, Andres Duany, Elizabeth Plater-Zyberk and Jeff Speck argue for a return to American vernacular architecture as a way out of the wasteland of cookie-cutter housing and poor street planning that typify suburbia as we know it. What is "new" about this urbanism is its version of "old." Harking back to the sort of suburban context for which Wright would have been building his Prairie Style houses, Duany and company assemble an impressive amount of material in support of their claim that suburbia is dysfunctional as an architectural community. Jacobs is cited with much approval, but there is something decidedly un-Jacobean about the idea that suburbia needs to be reformed at the implicit cost of rotted-out inner cities. It is true that the authors of *Suburban Nation* draw upon exurban space in some major cities for inspiration. But the communities built under the flag of vernacular New Urbanism are pretty disconnected from anything like a real city. New Urbanists would in effect correspond to the "decentrists" of Jacobs' book, even though New Urbanists will argue that they are not—not *really*. For they relocate the "center" to the town square and similar village concepts. Of course diverging from Jacobs might be all to the good, depending on cases. It is something of a vernacular New Urbanist tic to cite Jacobs, but waving her work around like a talisman won't get anybody anywhere.

What are Celebration and Seaside like? They are pleasant communities, whose houses are organized in terms of several New Urbanist principles. They are built in vernacular style with a great degree of stylistic coherence. Their traffic plans reject wide street corner radii adopted from highway planning and reassert four corners control for enhanced pedestrian safety. There are ample sidewalks to carry the pedestrian traffic and mixed-use zoning—mostly for retail shopping and community activity buildings—to allow the pedestrians to have somewhere other than each other's houses as destinations. The communities are centered on town squares in order to facilitate intercourse among the population, and vertical building is strictly limited in order to maintain a sense of dispersal among the various uses to which the towns are put. Garages are not visible from the front elevations of the houses and the houses themselves are tied intimately to the street— i.e., they are not set back centered on a large plot of land as are many large suburban homes (Figure 3.3).[16]

Sounds good, doesn't it? It is certainly better than the serpentine-streeted mega-suburbs familiar to many from their own experience and from watching too many Steven Spielberg movies. But there are a few questions to ask of this sort of planning. The first thing to notice is that the demographics of

Figure 3.3 Seaside, Florida [Jerry Sharp]

these communities are depressing. All good intent aside,[17] both Celebration and Seaside are overwhelmingly white and upper-middle class. U.S. Census figures for the year 2000 for Celebration were: 93.57 percent white, 2.41 percent Asian/ Asian-American, 1.72 percent African/African-American, and 0.26 percent Native American, with the remainder as "other." Income figures were slightly less discouraging: the average income was $77,231 per annum. The picture at Seaside is in many ways worse. It is quite small—around 650 residences— and unincorporated. There are, therefore, no census figures for it available. It was planned from the start as a vacation community on the upper Gulf Coast and, although the Panama City area may not be the most desirable beach front in Florida, the build cost and price were not cheap. Still, at first the houses were somewhat affordable and the architecture as a whole—Florida bungalow style—was convincingly indigenous. It is now an enclave of the wealthy (as is Greenwich

Village these days, to be fair) replete with seaside manses. The biggest beach front properties sell for well in the $2 to $5 million range and there is no lower income group represented at all. What seems to have begun as a vernacular community attracted many to its version of village life and with them the very real estate development forces for which Seaside was meant to be an antidote. To put it mildly, the chances for a diverse group of people spontaneously congregating at the town hall are slim to none, unless all that one means by "diverse" is "other people" or "people with different jobs." Community cohesiveness and diversity are supposed to go hand in hand in the New Urbanism; cohesiveness alone is not enough for community. Bernhard Förster's fascist experimental community Neuva Germania in Paraguay may have been as cohesive as one likes, the population at one with itself meeting in the town square for schnapps and sloganeering, but that is hardly what one wants out of an architecturally vibrant "community."[18] And, given even the right kind of coherence, it is an open question whether the smallish model communities of the New Urbanist ilk can withstand the colonizing influence of suburbanism and in this way encourage diversity.[19]

I live on West Washington Street in South Bend, Indiana, in the section of the city that was, at its industrial height, the most well-heeled. Many of the larger homes were built in the last twenty years of the nineteenth century in a style known as Stick or East Lake Victorian, but over the years several other sorts of architecture have also made an appearance: the Prairie Style Wright home I mentioned earlier, Queen Anne, Italianate, "Four Square," as well as two large mansions built in the fieldstone Gothic style that were home to generations of Studebakers. The street is not entirely domestic: there is a former orphanage building (now a former Head Start building), small businesses and industries, the Studebaker Museum, two funeral parlors, many imposing old churches, and two sizable low-income housing developments. Much of this fell to tatters in the Depression era and did not recover until reclaimed in the historic preservation movement in the latter part of the twentieth century. Before that time most of the domestic architecture was in use as brothels, speakeasies, gambling parlors, and crack houses. The area is ethnically and economically diverse. Perhaps, on a small scale, this is something like what Jacobs envisions by a "diverse" urban area.

To be fair, one can't just grow areas like West Washington Street from scratch. It may be wrong to task Seaside and Celebration with not having done so. Nevertheless, such planned communities do seem to work at a remove from the realities of urban ethical life that so engaged Jacobs. They are, along this dimension at least, unreal posits of architectural and urban form without much of the intended content of life that is supposed to surround them. It is not for nothing that the director Peter Weir chose Seaside as the shooting locale for his film *The Truman Show*. That movie, after all, was about a self-sealed simulacrum of a life, televised, unbeknownst to the title character, to the outside world as a reality TV show— a somewhat benign mix of Descartes' demon, Marshall McLuhan's glib dictum that "the medium is the message," and Huxley's dystopianism. Being picked as the ready-made context for that movie is not a good sign, if what one is after in building such a community is *real* community.

But what of less political questions of architectural experience in such places? Neither Seaside nor Celebration is as boring as track housing, but the architecture is extremely uniform. Although one can hear many terms used to refer to the stated aim of the lived experience of these buildings and their effects on the street life of the community, one term that is often used is "comfort."[20] Of course, there is nothing wrong with certain things that might come under that heading: safe streets and houses, for instance. Nor would one want to fall into the formalist trap of denying livability in favor of form or function, even if the form or function in question is sensitive to the idea of the lived body. But if by "comfort" one means something like "satiation," that once again raises the issue of the degree to which architecture is merely *reactive* to habitual ways of experiencing space or whether at least part of its purpose is to introduce new modes of such experience. The latter is a guiding idea for much architectural modernism but, because of the checkered history of the application of the idea to concrete building practices, the very idea has suffered a black eye. Poor past application of an idea, of course, is no argument against the idea itself. As we saw in Chapter 1, there are many issues here. In some of the main representatives of what might be now called "classical" modernism—Le Corbusier, Mies, Gropius, even Wright—an imbalance has been at work in favor of what some critics call "ocularcentrism,"[21] i.e., the idea that sight is the main modality of architectural experience.[22] As I argued in Chapter 1, this is a mistake if what an architect wants to do is engage embodied experience of spatiality in global terms. New Urbanism as it stands at least unconsciously buys into ocularcentrism. We also saw in our discussion of the work of the proceduralists that the degree to which human embodied response to architectural surrounds is "plastic"—i.e., the degree to which it can be changed—is a matter of some controversy. Sheer human physicality surely places some modes of experience out of the realm of possibility. Still, one should feel uncomfortable with armchair *a priori* setting of limitations. The potential for engaging deep human architectural response is likely not tapped out and comfort cannot remain unanalyzed as an imperative. A bit of initial discomfort can spur one on to deeper stabilities and urban and architectural responsiveness. There may even be a place for radical disorientation in testing the limits of response. One might not domicile oneself in the most challenging urban landscapes; nevertheless, they may form a very important part of the architectural continuum. New Urbanists are fond of explaining the abiding appeal of Walt Disney World in Florida in terms of its small town feel (surely too simple an explanation, but leave it at that). How much more fun, architecturally speaking, to have one's embodied sense of self stretched by playing in any number of more experimental buildings and built surroundings, in which the architecture is the ride and not just something next to the ticketed attractions.

One cannot help but form the impression, at least at this stage of the game, that New Urbanism is only New Suburbanism, and thus not a proper descendant of Jacobs. It is also a new type of formalism. This is an especially painful charge for the New Urbanist to bear, since the whole purpose of the movement was to reintroduce into the modern context a new ethical dimension to architecture. That is, New Urbanism was supposed to be *anti-formalist*. One cause of this return to formalism *malgré lui* is the lack of a deep aesthetics and, thus, of a viable connection between experience and ethics. By deep aesthetics I mean a theoretically articulated appreciation that human perceptual capacities are to be engaged by and in architecture in every corner of those capacities. Ocularism in contrast is a "surface aesthetics" that emphasizes "look," by which I mean disembodied visual experience. Ocularism—which I believe is part and parcel of the New Urbanism—doesn't even get visual experience right, i.e., one cannot merely add to ocularism more engagement with other sense modalities and end up with an adequate account of architectural experience. The outcome of just doing that is to create something on the order of a movie set for living, opening oneself up to the observation, made by Gertrude Stein of her hometown of Oakland, California, that "there is no there there." New Urbanism, as it now stands, has merely grafted an ethics of the small town onto the unquestioned assumptions of the precedence of the ocular in architecture, as one would expect, given its vernacular basis.

ETHICS AND EXPERIENCE IN MASS BUILDING

The phenomenological assessment of Seaside and Celebration cannot be merely one of taste—that they are boring, don't look right, or are too comfy. It is one, rather, that brings to bear a demand for a deeper connection between ethics and embodied perception. Except in its infancy as a form of philosophical methodology geared toward a foundational role for the sciences, phenomenology of different stripes has tried to establish just this kind of connection—Merleau-Ponty, Sartre, Lévinas and, although he denied it, even Heidegger, sought something like it.[23] But the marriage between phenomenology on the one hand and ethics on the other has been fraught with tensions of various sorts. Most of these are due to the way the systematic peculiarities of phenomenological work of different philosophers comport with the structure of their ethical views. There is nothing that inherently bars phenomenology and ethics from a substantial relationship.

One can ask the question of the connection of phenomenology of architecture to ethics in two idioms. The first we have already posed and addressed. Here ethics has an extended meaning of "care to provide conditions for valued life." Clearly architecture that is sensitive to embodied perceptual response will have ethical value in this sense. So long as it is a value of the good life to move in such spaces, there will be ethical value in such buildings. If the question is put in narrower terms, the connection between ethics and the phenomenology of architecture is more difficult to make out. This narrower sense of the term will involve treating ethics as something along the lines of a moral way of life. The second idiom trades on this more specific sense of ethics.

No arrangement of buildings in a total built environment will determine or even help determine any particular set of ethical beliefs or action over and against any other set. Of course buildings can express or exemplify ideas, some of them ethical, and such expression does occur at primary levels of experience such as perception. Once ideas are in place in a culture, they may be in place in the modality of architecture. It is also the case, of course, that architecture can further solidify the hold certain ideas have in a culture by expressing them and that, in turn, some of these ideas may be ethical. We have already mentioned this in a concrete example—i.e., the existing Beaux Arts structure of the Nelson-Atkins Museum. Other cases are more spectacular, and regrettable. Take an especially egregious example: Albert Speer's plans for central Berlin to make it the worthy capital of the Third Reich. So redolent of Nazism are the buildings that it is hard to credit the idea that, even though their phenomenological meaning was determined in fact by fascism, it needn't have been. That is, it is compatible with its phenomenology that the plan might have expressed some other (pretty bland and overly formalistic) ethical regime. There is no royal road leading from the phenomenology of architecture to one kind of ethics. One already has ethical concepts or attitudes in play in perception, and the phenomenologist will show how they interact with non-ethical aspects of perception. It is true that some phenomenologists attempt to generate what are sometimes termed meta-ethical concepts or constraints out of non-ethical phenomenological analysis of primary modes of being with other humans—resulting in categories like "the Other," "the They," etc.—but such analyses are tendentious in their details and move well beyond what is necessary for the general phenomenological reorientation towards architecture we have thus far discussed.

Instead of arguing for a particular substantive ethical theory with a phenomenological basis, I would like to discuss what may seem to be at first a pretty unpromising alternative in making out the connection between phenomenological, sensitive architecture and the narrower sense of "ethics" identified above. It will seem so because this approach might be taken to be a retrenchment in the very formalism that we have been trying to avoid. In fact, the connection between the phenomenology and ethics of architecture that I shall turn to does not result in or depend upon formalism in either phenomenology or in ethics, but it does argue for a connection between the phenomenology and ethics of architecture at a far more general level and in a more indirect way than is usual.

Take the idea of phenomenological richness that we have developed over the course of the book. Assume that you don't view ethics as a system of rule promulgation and following, where the idea of a "rule" is something like a law. If you don't, some philosophers like Aristotle, Hegel, Adorno, Foucault, Alasdair MacIntyre, Charles Taylor, and Bernard Williams have suggested in their different ways that you might shift your understanding of the nature of ethical judgment. If one views it as, in the first instance at least, not involving rule application, one is free to see ethical judgment more as a skill, in which ways of acting or thinking are taken to be proper to the given contexts for which action or thought are pertinent. One can, of course, say general things about how to act— many judgments about not killing innocents are apt to come out the same way across the board. This is because the subject matter of some ethical judgments may be less context-dependent than others. But no ethical judgment is entirely abstract; there is always some context sensitivity. If this is a viable way to think about ethical life, one can see how perceptual abilities—and embodied ones at that—would be crucial to ethics. On this understanding of the nature of judgment, being able to attend to the infinitely complex gradations in situations, motivations, character traits, etc. would be paramount. Only with such an ability can one appreciate a given context for what it is. Developing this subtlety of perception along with a sharp critical impulse has sometimes been considered the province of art and its appreciation. It's easy to see why many think of the nineteenth-century novel in this way. Flaubert was a master at developing multifaceted perceptual responses to his work by the careful cultivation of ethical ambiguity. Even the tedious Henry James is interesting, to a degree, along this dimension.

One might immediately object that this increase in perceptual acuity and imagination, even if it does improve ethical response, is not unique to architecture or perhaps even to art. One might develop this perceptiveness from viewing a painting, hearing a cantata, or reading a sestina. Even so, the sense of being embodied with these arts is arguably less pronounced, so that, if what one wants is a tie between ethics and embodied perceptual acuity, architecture seems most pertinent. A second concern might be that this indirect connection holds between architectural perception and ethics, not the ethics of architecture as such. But the ethics of architecture as posed in Chapter 3 by our consideration of urban planning and total architecture has put the point of the ethics of architecture in precisely this way—as a matter of ethics more generally.

Epilogue

Architecture is in many ways unrivaled as an art. Buildings stand the test of time in ways that easel art, books, and music can only envy. There are limits of course. Shelley's "Ozymandias" warns that renown breaks hard on the rock of ages, that:

> Nothing beside remains. Round the decay
> Of that colossal wreck, boundless and bare
> The lone and level sands stretch far away.

Notwithstanding, the artistic production of the most ancient cultures has its prime extant form in architecture. Architecture also deals in art of great scope, promising (or threatening) a sort of total experience of art that has attracted megalomania as well as sensitive planning of the urban landscape. Such massive building implicates yet another aspect of architecture that takes it out of the artistic ordinary—its cost. Only the making and marketing of major Hollywood films can currently compete with public architecture in terms of the amount of monetary resources that must be committed in order to bring artistic intent to fruition. And this means that buildings express whatever is expressed about social will, at least when it comes to capital as a signal of that will. Those who pay for architecture generally like to have a say in it and some very complex projects—witness the plan for rebuilding the World Trade Center site—can involve a cacophony of moneyed voices, sometimes in direct competition with an architect's initial main vision for the project. Even those—perhaps mostly those—who are in the population at large, and on whom building will impact experientially the most as an expression of general political will, also have an interest in having their views heard. The situation with domestic architecture is a bit less demanding, but it is still the case that a house is likely to be the most expensive thing a homeowner buys in her lifetime.

Because architecture has such broad significance generally it can seem intractable to any one understanding of that significance. One way to deal with this intractability—to rationalize it away, in effect—is to try to reduce the significance of architecture to a form of artistic meaning that seems more tractable. I have argued that this path of despair is not mandatory and that, by succumbing to it, we can miss a whole range of meaning that is constitutive of architecture. For taking the path typically ends one up in thinking about architecture in terms of criteria developed in other visual arts and this, in turn, results in architectural formalism.

Each of the three chapters of this book has treated a different aspect of the significance of architecture by resisting the despairing reduction. The first chapter discussed a different basis for understanding the perceptual experience of architecture by introducing into the evaluation the idea of embodied experience. Architecture places demands upon embodied experience in a way no other art does. Although one hesitates to call anything the essence of anything nowadays, it would be difficult to imagine architecture that did not take the embodied experience of it to be tremendously important. Chapter 2 turned to questions of the hierarchical relation of architecture to other arts, analogic relations between architecture and other arts that both cast architecture in terms of those other arts and vice versa, and relations between architecture and other arts in terms of the concept of architectural space. This investigation deepened the sense in which architecture fares well or ill with respect to the arts generally, and pressed deeper into the problems that can result from not according architecture its proper autonomy. Of course, the story is not all negative—there are plenty of ways to think of architecture in terms of aspects of other arts that need not be reductive, but one must be careful with the analogies. The final chapter turned yet again to issues of the place of architecture in more general built environments. Questions of site specificity, the role of architecture in building and maintaining community, and the ethics of architecture were at issue. Here questions of architectural formalism—under the banner of "ocularity"—pointedly resurfaced. As it turns out, some prominent attempts to reinsert ethics into architecture operate with such a thin idea of the experience of architecture (see Chapter 1) that they replicate the formalism that they meant to replace. Put in Freudian terms, they displace it instead of replace it. Such planned communities tend toward nostalgia rather than toward elaborating communal richness.

Part of what can be worthwhile in considering the relation of architecture to some of its kindred arts, to return a last time to the subject matter of Chapter 2, is that one can develop an appreciation of the idea of architectural space in contexts other than architecture. Some of these contexts are, simply put, more controllable and suggestive than constructing a major building. Even a rather unlikely candidate, film— as our consideration of Wenders' *Wings of Desire* showed —can investigate architectural space in ways that sharpen our understanding of the architectural space *of architecture*. Because media differ, ways that architectural space is present in other artistic domains can differ substantially from the standard architectural case and, when placed back within the architectural context, can become especially arresting and inspirational. The case can be reversed: architectural space as a formal element of a film can influence ideas of what is possible within the medium of film.

I have not meant this book to be one continuous argument; it is rather a series of (I hope complicated and interesting) snapshots to get one thinking about architecture and its autonomy. But central casting has supplied an elephant for the room, and that is architectural formalism. Some might think—have thought—that formalism just comes as part and parcel with modernism. And why should modernist architecture be any different? But there is an important distinction to make here. Even if it is the case that modernism has, as a matter of its history, courted formalism in one of its many forms, this does not entail that it needs to do so. What would be required in order to establish this stronger claim is some sort of argument to the effect that there are elements necessary to modernism that are conceptually incompatible with modernism not being formalistic. But there are no such arguments. A building like Holl's Nelson-Atkins Museum can be both modernist and non-formalist.

Standard reactions against architectural formalism make just this mistake: they assume that a rejection of formalism requires a rejection of modernism. Typically, then, they replace the idea central to modernism that experience is something the limits of which have not been determined, let alone reached, with a version of the past. The recuperation of these past versions usually papers over some of the reasons that they became past versions in the first place. Ironically, perhaps, anti-modern reactions against formalism tend to replicate formalism within themselves. This is easily explained. Modernist formalism did not condense out of thin air. It was a distillation of varieties of formalism that held sway in architecture for centuries. When the anti-modernists retreat to that tradition they are, therefore, not being anti-formalist at all. This means that their stated purpose of marrying architecture with ethics will face all the challenges that beset formalist theories of architecture. Concurrently, formal modernism has become a style that has *retrouvé* appeal, but the sloganeering tokened by "form follows function," "less is more," "a machine for living," and "ornament is crime" is dead. No one today would throw a Barcelona chair on the barricades (Mies wouldn't have either!).

Some of the most invigorating architects and architectural historians and critics embrace anti-formalist modernism by keeping the idea of embodied experience specifically in mind. But it is still too early to tell if this is a growing trend even in public architecture, not to mention whether ideas developed in the public realm will trickle down into less "advanced" building. But it is encouraging that one can gain enough distance from pre-modern, modern *and* post-modern varieties of formalism to pose again questions of how it is that what one might have thought were purely formal qualities of architecture can implicate and forward our other material engagements.

1 The phenomenological approach that I discuss can have social components and implications. But the social elements tend to be less prominent than in some other approaches to the question of the meaning of architecture or its material concerns. And so, for instance, I shall not treat the very important idea of "social space" inaugurated by Lefebvre 1991 [1974]. The exclusion of this topic is especially significant for Chapter 3, which treats certain themes at the intersection of the experience of architecture and urbanism. My rationale for the exclusion is twofold. First, many Lefebvre-inspired accounts take on board very complex political commitments (in Lefevbre's own case, structural Marxism) that I cannot adequately address in a book of this scope. Second, the idea of social space—while having application to architectural space—is far broader than that, extending for instance to conceptions of geographical space and other matters outside the direct purview of architecture. Again, consideration of this sort of view would take us off track. Other views that I do treat that have clear social-scientific components are both more narrowly related to architecture and its urban effects and easier to detach from their background theoretical commitments.

2 See, e.g., Goodman 1988.

ONE   BODIES AND ARCHITECTURAL SPACE

1 See Harries 1998 and Norberg-Schulz 1985 and 1990, both largely following Heidegger 1962 and 1971, pp. 143–62.

2 There is a rich vein of thought outside the context of twentieth-century French philosophy that also treats the concept of being

embodied. See especially O'Shaughnessy 1980 and 2003, Hurley 1998, and Noë 2006.

3 Gutting 2001, p. 185.

4 Merleau-Ponty, following Heidegger, denies that this can be done purely, i.e., without interpretation entering into the description at all. Increasingly, Merleau-Ponty's work admits historical, cultural, and dialectical dimensions. Some of this is already present in his earlier work as well.

5 Heidegger 1962, p. 4ff.; cf. Skinner 1953; Quine 1960, ch. 3. Whether Quine was a behaviorist and, if he was, in what sense, is a subject of disagreement among his readers and disciples. For Dreyfus, see Dreyfus 1991.

6 The idea that breakdowns in basic everyday orientation reveal important aspects of those structures that would otherwise go unremarked is, again, one Merleau-Ponty takes from Heidegger.

7 This is a bit unfair to Descartes. First of all, the "I think" (*cogito/je pense*) is one of many possible first-person thoughts that can stand as basic. He means it to be a catch-all category broad enough for all of them, e.g., "I doubt," "I wish," etc. It is also true that Descartes writes that the mind is not in the body like a "pilot is in a ship." But, while the *thought* "I act" would qualify as basic, *acting* would not.

8 There is another, more religious, way to frame the issue that is relevant to Merleau-Ponty. What is missing from the English term is a meaning implicated in the Greek–Latin origin of "chair" (from the words $\kappa\rho\acute{\epsilon}\alpha\varsigma$ and *caro*, respectively)—i.e., *incarnation*. Roughly, the idea seems to be that the experience of the body in the world is one in which the body is suffused with mind analogous to the way it is said that the Christian God joins and thoroughly transfigures Christ as simultaneously fully divine and human.

9 The case of the connection between taste and smell is special. Taste seems especially influenced by smell. Physiologists typically claim that the tongue can only discern four tastes: sweet, sour, salty, and bitter. All apparent differentiation within those categories, as well as savory sensations that extend beyond them, is due to the influence of smell on taste. The childhood practice of holding one's nose while taking medicine has a purpose, if the influence of smell creates an especially disgusting taste. Because the dependence of taste on smell is a default state of

human sensation and not exceptional, psychologists do not treat it as true synaesthesia.

10 Pallasmaa 2005.

11 Haptic experience becomes an important object of analysis with phenomenology, but there are pre-phenomenological considerations of the topic. Most notable is J.G. Herder, who developed the idea that touch could be allied to visual modalities in his interpretation of the general character of sculpture. See the "Fourth Grove" of his *Critical Forests*, excerpted in Herder 2006.

12 Pallasmaa 2005, p. 18 (Plate 2).

13 Sometimes one finds claims that Merleau-Ponty was the first phenomenologist to consider the question of kinaesthesis or, even more broadly, the idea of embodiedness. This is false. Husserl had been concerned with both these issues from the mid-first decade of the twentieth century onwards. His most sustained discussion is in *Ideas II*, volume 4 of Husserl 1956– (Husserl calls this the experience of the *Ich-Leib*). For the discussion of kinaestheisis, see Husserl 1973, § 19.

14 How early in the cognitive process concepts enter into experience is the subject of much debate in the philosophy of mind and language. We can't canvass the possibilities here, but phenomenological approaches to consciousness will characteristically argue for a very early entry of categorization into experience. The concepts or categories may not be very explicitly deployed, but it is hard, if not impossible, so the phenomenologist will claim, to isolate in experience conceptual from non-conceptual content. A related issue involves the degree to which such concepts and categories are natural and the degree to which they are social. That there is no natural kind of "liberty" seems clear. The concept is a human invention to refer to a property of human social life. Its source is social and, if the concept does structure thought perceptually, it will do so from a social basis. The concept of triangularity does not seem to be social at all. This is not to say that it cannot have or participate in particular social meanings—for instance in Pythagorean mysticism or dynastic Egyptian architecture, etc.—but it doesn't seem correct to hold that seeing a closed three-sided figure requires one to be in a specific culture at a specific time. Both sorts of concepts operate in the experience of architecture. The phenomenology of architecture will open out to its social dimensions along these two paths: (a) through

embodied experience mediated by social categories and concepts, and (b) through embodied experience mediated by non-social categories and concepts, if those categories and concepts have conceptual linkage to social understandings of them. As it turns out, in architecture the conditional (b) is almost always met.

15 The classic treatments are von Simson 1956, pp. 50ff. and Panofsky 1946. In allowing that medieval aesthetics of light is an aesthetics of beauty I am in disagreement with Eco 1986, pp. 13–14 (following Huizinga 1965, pp. 254ff.). I believe the concept of beauty is capacious enough, historically speaking, to accommodate the example.

16 *De consecratione ecclesiae santi Dionysii* in Suger 1867 documents the construction.

17 The best treatment of shadow known to me is Baxandall 1995.

18 Dates following buildings or projects are, unless indicated, dates of completion.

19 Scruton 1979, ch. 4; cf. Rasmussen 1959.

20 For an example of this approach that received quite a lot of press attention when published, see Wolfe 1981.

21 De Botton 2006.

22 Holl 1989, p. 10; Holl 1996, p. 15.

23 Holl 1989, p. 10.

24 Holl 1989, p. 12; Holl 1996, p. 12.

25 Holl 1989, p. 10.

26 Holl 1996, p. 13.

27 Cf. the first concept drawings of the space in Holl 2000, pp. 258ff. It is revealing to compare this use of parallax to the technique of *passage*—the elision of planes in painterly space—in the work of Cézanne, Braque, and Picasso. *Passage* allows the artist to merge planes by leaving single edges unpainted or lighter in tone. One might argue that this is an adaptation of architectural space within the space of painting. In the case of Holl, the adaptation comes full circle back into architecture.

28 See Holl 1996, p. 11.

29 So-called after the short-lived literary magazine L=A=N=G=U=A=G=E, edited by Charles Bernstein from 1978 to 1981. Language poetry attempts to structure poems so that they must be "completed" by the interpretative interventions of their readers. Emphasis is placed both on verbal inventiveness with everyday speech and reader disorientation.

The roots of the movement are many: the Objectivist poetry of Charles Olson and Louis Zukofsky, the more lyrical strand of the Black Mountain School like Robert Creeley, as well as Frank O'Hara and William Carlos Williams. Madeline Gins' *What the President Will Say and Do!!* (1984) and *Helen Keller or Arakawa* (1994) are seminal works in the movement.

30 Gins & Arakawa 2002, ch. 5.

31 Ibid., p. 21.

32 The *locus classicus* that explores this thought is Bachelard 1969 [1957].

TWO ARCHITECTURE AND OTHER ARTS

1 Kristeller 1951–2.

2 See Ruskin 1989 [1880], ch. 3 and, especially the "Nature of Gothic" in the useful abridgement of *The Stones of Venice*, Ruskin 1960 [1853], pp. 157–90.

*3 Schopenhauer tethers art to a metaphysical task. He does this along two dimensions, one having to do with the alleged origin of art and the other having to do with its cognitive role in human life. Like all else for Schopenhauer, art is an expression in the phenomenal realm of the all-encompassing Will, the prime force whose activity is not only non-phenomenal but, in ways that cannot be conceptually fathomed, determines what there is to experience phenomenally. What is special about art—and this idea is shared with Schelling, who had it first—is that it is a product of human phenomenal action that displays more of a share of its origin in Will than do other more theoretical products. In a sense, art is humanity's best attempt to bend itself back on its own origin, which origin is always beyond its grasp. For this reason art is both tragic and revelatory at the same time: tragic because it displays the gap between humans and a suffering-free origin (in which there is no individuation and, therefore, strictly speaking no "life" either); revelatory because it also provides within human experience the best attempt at escape velocity, i.e., at transcending the phenomenal realm.

Most who study Schopenhauer find this concept of the Will (and several other concepts that he places beside it, e.g., that of Platonic Ideas) incoherent. Nonetheless, Schopenhauer more than any other German philosopher actually influenced the way artists made art works in the latter part of the nineteenth and earlier part of the twentieth centuries. His very low opinion of architecture relative to the other arts is, therefore, worth understanding. Arts, for him, can be typed in terms of the basic phenomenal forces that they depend upon for their effects, which forces are themselves emanations of the cosmic Will. The more basic the forces, the more they are bound to the phenomenal realm, and the more they are so bound, the less they can point beyond it. Architecture deals with forces of gravity and, more particularly, with the struggle between ascending structure and being bound to the earth by gravity (Schopenhauer 1969 [1819/44], I: 214, 255; II: 411ff.) It is the polar opposite of music—the *sine qua non* of Schopenhauer's vocation of art as a means for temporary and approximate liberation from the slings and arrows of bodily existence. The "sole analogy" of music to architecture is in terms of their metrics. In music this is rhythm and in architecture symmetry (ibid., II: 453).

*4 Hegel's attitudes towards architecture are also products of a general metaphysical picture about the significance of the various arts. In some ways, his views are an extension of Schelling's, with whom he was friends before falling out in 1807. More particularly, Hegel's views are complicated by a bifurcated system of assessing the arts that is an heir to Schelling's treatment, but takes that treatment in a new direction. For Schelling's views, see note 7 below.

Hegel was committed to a progressive view of the development of the arts in various historical epochs. Any type of art must be assessed along two dimensions for Hegel. First, it must be understood in terms of the point in the conceptual history of humanity at which it claims the greatest extent of its power to organize human understanding. Hegel claims that art in general reached this height of influence in Attic Greece and that the arts ascendant at that time—sculpture and tragic drama—are the most important arts, if what one is concerned with is the question of art's power as a form of knowledge. Past that time, art can no longer be at the forefront of human understanding because human understanding deploys means more adequate to the evolving requirements of human self-understanding. Hegel holds that there are three main forms of art as a form of cognition: "classical" art already mentioned, "symbolic" art, which is relatively primitive and bound to attempts to inadequately portray the divine in the sensuous world, and "romantic" art, which dates from the Hellenistic period to Hegel's own time. Architecture is the supreme representative of symbolic art—the

Great Pyramid is one of Hegel's prime examples (Hegel 1975 [1835], pp. 354–57, 632, 650–54). This pegs architecture as an early and inadequate art form. A second way that Hegel assesses the individual arts is to judge them relative to all three periods. Architecture doesn't just stop with Egyptian art, after all—there are Greek temples, medieval churches, and Baroque *Rathäuser*. Because it is an expression of human self-understanding that is inherently wed to non-representational yet material articulation, architecture slips further in its ability to keep pace with the sophistication of human knowledge up to the romantic period. So, in Hegel's own time, it is ranked quite low indeed (ibid., pp. 83ff., 633–34, 684ff.)

5 It would not have occurred to these philosophers at all that non-built representations of buildings could count as architecture, as some theorists think today. See Tschumi 1996, pp. 66–78. Given the vagaries that govern whether a planned building will be built, it is perhaps understandable why competition plans would count as architecture in some estimations. They are certainly work, but the problem of whether they constitute architectural *works* is a complicated one that I cannot do justice to here. For a cursory glance at some of the issues, see Goodman 1988 and 1976, pp. 218–21.

6 Schelling 1989 [1859], pp. 165–66, 177; Goethe, a bit later, also makes the claim. The German participial adjective *erstarrte* means "stiffened" or "solidified." There is a figurative use of the word in connection with flowing liquid that is best rendered "frozen." Because the idea that music has a flowing character is a commonplace in both English and German, I opt for the more figurative translation.

*7 Schelling begins a trend in nineteenth-century philosophy of thinking of the value of art in terms of its ability to display for humans aspects of their natures that systematically elude more theoretical understanding and yet remain cognitively essential. The overarching aim of Schelling's early thinking was to explicate the emergence of intelligence from what he called anorganic (i.e., inorganic) nature and lower forms of organic nature in a way that did justice to the fact that the meaning of that emergence for humans has a peculiar reflexive structure. It is part of the emergence that the emergence be understood, which understanding will require speculation concerning the origin from which the emergence stems in terms that are outside the province of the origin.

Although it needn't concern us, these have to do with a system of forces of forming and being formed, or of universality and particularity, that Schelling develops at great length in an earlier book, *Ideas for a Philosophy of Nature* (1797). But the broad concern about the proper form of understanding of matters that are conditions for conceptual articulation is a completely standard problem in German Idealism after Kant. Schelling is a primary exponent of seeing art as the key to such an understanding (as were, in their own ways, Schopenhauer and the early Nietzsche).

Schelling confuses many by talking about various types of art on two different levels with two different attendant sets of meanings. On the more metaphysical level, he divides art according to what he calls its "forms" into music, painting, and plastic arts based on an arcane metaphysical formula involving "the principle of indifference." These forms of art are something like Platonic forms or concepts of formative activity in art and not the various arts—e.g., the art of music, the art of painting, etc.—themselves. Those arts can each realize (or not realize) to various degrees within them the basic formative types of art so that, e.g., a painting, a genre of painting, or even painting as such has shares of music. To take one of Schelling's own examples, in the art type "music," the formal musical element is rhythm, the formal painting element is harmony, and the formal plastic constituent is melody (Schelling 1989 [1859], p. 162).

This structure, in turn, allows Schelling to think of the analogies between what we would take as different kinds of art as instances of sharing of the basic forms (or sometimes of subsidiary forms) of art between those kinds. This allows him to hold, for instance, that "the music within plastic arts is architecture" (ibid., p. 163). What this means is that the art kind "architecture" is the expression of the art form "music" within another art form "plastic art." It is a very rich structural notion of analogy, based in nested whole–part relations, no matter how speculative its content may seem.

Architecture for Schelling is to be understood, as all art is to be understood, as encapsulating this process of cosmic formation. Different art forms exhibit different degrees of stress on one of the components as present in either the "real" or the "ideal." Ideal art is art that is able explicitly to express thoughts, i.e., "art of speech." Real art is art that sensuously exemplifies components of thought and, thus, the basic forces, and can be subdivided into arts that deal in organic or inorganic modalities. In fact, all real arts exemplify both modalities, but in different equilibria and to different degrees. Music involves mostly anorganic processes, namely the completely general relation of unity to multiplicity within the domain of the real. Strictly speaking, there are no musical objects, on the assumption, made by Schelling, that "objects" in this sense require formed *matter*. The "force-domain," if one can coin a phrase, within the real to which music corresponds is magnetism. Painting is the art that does have objects proper, and its corresponding force is light.

Schelling states that architecture is the organic form of art *par excellence*. By this he seems to mean that it deals with the most material complexity within a unity and thus exhibits organic structure more than do other modalities of art. Moreover, the organic form that architecture takes is plant-like. But he holds that the significance of architecture is that it moves back to anorganicity from the organic. Schelling links this to the natural process of making over an environment in terms of impulse that is shared between humans and certain animals (ibid., p. 163). This impulse is but a special case of a more general formative impulse that extends back into non-intelligent organic nature according to Schelling. He cites bees making combs and the reproductive impulse as examples. The key point here is that the stuff of the making comes from the maker, e.g., the bees produce the inorganic material for their cells from within themselves and give significance to it (i.e., bring it back into the sphere of organic purposes) by using it over again. The idea is that intelligence is but a highly articulated special case of this activity and that art is the special case within the special case that shows this structure of movement from the organic to the anorganic and back most explicitly.

All the arts that deal with the domain of the real are, in a sense, inferior to the more thought-conducive arts of ideality. So, architecture will rank below poetry, drama, and, perhaps, opera. It also seems to rank as a plastic art below sculpture, which exhibits a superior equilibrium between organicity and anorganicity. But architecture does outstrip music and painting in what matters most to Schelling. For architecture deals better with the cohabitation of form and matter in the real world. Schelling's view is seen quite appropriately as a bit of an advance over

Kant in the career of music on its path to becoming the main art in terms of which the other arts are modeled in the nineteenth century. But only just—his emphasis on the plastic arts betrays reliance on Winckelmann and, although poetry will continue to claim its share of the limelight in views of subsequent idealists (under the rubric of lyric poetry, i.e., musical poetry) his rating of poetry above all other arts is also a remnant of the cultural envy Germans felt towards French neo-classicism.

8 Kivy argues that there is a more interesting kind of representation that occurs much more frequently in music, in which ideas or emotions are expressed through musical representation of aspects of the world. His example is the third movement from Beethoven's *Pastoral Symphony*, "Szene am Bach." As the title to the movement indicates, one is given over to hearing the rhythm of the music as a babbling brook and to experiencing the gaiety characteristic of the scene in those terms. See Kivy 1984, ch. 7.

9 Of course sound is a physical phenomenon that requires space, and architecture exists in time. Sometimes it is even built with an eye to its aging in a variety of ways. On the latter, see Mostafavi & Leatherbarrow 1993.

*10 See Kant 1928 [1790], pp. 42ff. That Kant is an arch-representatialist about art cannot be seriously doubted. Things are more complex when it comes to the concept of disinterest. Kant's ranking of architecture among its artistic rivals can seem to single out architecture's pragmatic function as problematic for it and determine its status in terms of unease with it as a suitable object of disinterest. But Kant's view is subtler than this. The impression that Kant is not architecture-friendly stems from his use of an example of a rudimentary hut to illustrate impermissible mixing of considerations of the uses of an object in pure aesthetic judgment. What is sometimes missed in discussions of Kant's use of the example of the hut is that it is a simple hut devoid of beauty, not of necessity but just because it is so. It does not follow from this example (and Kant was famously suspicious of the use of examples in philosophy for just this reason) that architecture cannot be beautiful or otherwise artistically worthy at all. The better way to put Kant's point is that this particular illustration doesn't involve *architecture*, unless what "architecture" means is just "buildings." Generally speaking, taking account of the function of an object does not disqualify that object from being beautiful—Kant has a whole set of distinctions that are geared towards preserving this possibility—although it does mean that, in some sense, they are not as beautiful as less functional (beautiful) things. Even this last point is slippery, however.

Even so, it is the case that consideration of an object's function in a case of aesthetic judgment does create a more complex and less "pure" case of beauty, and Kant tends to rates beauties in terms of their purity. But when one turns to the sections of the *Critique of Judgement* that treat the ranking of architecture, there are surprises. There are two relevant sections: (1) § 51, in which Kant sets out a typology of the major divisions of the "fine arts," as he calls them, and (2) § 53, where he assigns a rank ordering, given the typology. Calling the arts typed in § 51 species of "fine art," as the English translation has it, is stipulative for Kant. The German phrase *schöne Kunst* means "beautiful art," Kant's main subject matter. All that Kant is interested in here is ordering arts in terms of their particular modes of presenting beauty. Architecture is a "formative" art, in which "semblance" to other objects in the world is not at issue (as it would be for painting, according to Kant). This groups architecture with sculpture as "plastic" arts that express "truth" by intuitive, sensuous means. What differentiates architecture from sculpture within the category of plastic arts is that its usefulness "controls" the expression of its artistic ideas (ibid., p. 186).

When one turns to the rank-ordering of the arts relative to one another, one finds Kant placing the formative arts (painting, sculpture, and architecture) smack in the middle, with the arts of speech (poetry and rhetoric) above and the art of the "play of sensations" (i.e., music and the "art of color") below. The principle of the ordering has nothing to do with how much use is implicated in the consideration of the object, although that concept does seem to play a continued role in how the arts are, pretty implicitly and vaguely, ranked within ranks (e.g., painting vs. architecture). Rather, the principle of ranking seems to be the degree to which the feeling of pleasure accompanying aesthetic reflection persists or not. Music is fleeting and so is valued less; poetry sticks with one (one can recite it and conjure the effect again, etc.). Architecture, apparently, lies between these poles (ibid., p. 195).

Kant is quick to warn that his ordering of the arts is conjectural and that there might be good arguments for other rankings (ibid., p. 184 n.1). It is interesting that, unlike other philosophers who knew much, much more than Kant about art, Kant does not venture an analysis of the all-important idea of genre or of the relation of different genres within or across the various artistic media. As far as architecture is concerned, Kant has almost nothing to say that is worthwhile to the phenomenologist of bodily experience. He states that design is paramount to architecture, that it is valuable as art in terms of its beauty, etc. (ibid., p. 67). Architecture is, for Kant, eye-candy. It is somewhat ironic perhaps that the one major idealist philosopher who ranks architecture highest relative to the other arts also exhibits the most shop-worn beautifying views on its essential nature. Once the idealists take architecture seriously, it suffers in comparison.

11 Schopenhauer is an interesting exception to the general trend in the period to place poetry at the top of the list, on the basis of the unity of music and language. See note 3 above. The young Nietzsche was very impressed by this view, as was Wagner in a way.

12 I do tax Kant with this last thought. See note 10 above.

13 The idea that architecture ought to be organic and, specifically, plant-like, is one of Schelling's favorites. See note 7 above.

14 "Fun" (i.e., the autonomous social aim of play) is a very important concept for understanding whole strands of thinking about the social and educative role of art from Kant onward. It is too bad that there is almost nothing written on this subject.

15 Krauss 1991.

16 See Sennett 1994, pp. 106–11.

17 Matta-Clark's connection to Earth Art also dates to his Cornell days. The White Museum at the university staged the epochal "Earth Art" exhibition in 1969, which was a signal event in the history of the development and critical reception of Earth Art and included important early works by the most important representative of that movement, Robert Smithson. Matta-Clark had graduated with his B.Arch. degree the prior year but returned to Ithaca to volunteer to stage the show. Matta-Clark's own work from the late 1960s shows a marked allegiance to many of the principles guiding the Earth Art movement.

18 Fried 1967. For the concept of absorption, see Fried 1980.

19 Fried's continuing interest in the power of genre for self-definition of

art has two main intellectual sources as far as I can tell: the essays of Clement Greenberg, whose criticism Fried knew well and valued highly in his youth, and the work of the philosopher Stanley Cavell.

20 Frank is best known for his photography, especially for his iconic collection *The Americans*. His most famous film is the seldom seen erotic documentary of the Rolling Stones' 1972 American tour, *Cocksucker Blues*. Apparently Mick Jagger doesn't like it very much and has blocked its release.

21 The striking difference between Matta-Clark and artists like Serra and Turrell, who I have claimed also seek phenomenological effects from their work, is in what one might call the tone of the work. There is a fair degree to which both Serra and Turrell attempt to control phenomenological responses to their work—sometimes to the point where one might even say one could have an "incorrect" or at least "inapt" response to it. Matta-Clark's work is not like this at all. It is much more joyful and accepting of various reactions to it. It is a kind of phenomenological "carnivalesque," to adapt the famous idea from the Russian literary theorist Mikhail Bakhtin.

22 Krauss 1985, pp. 262–74.

23 Ibid., pp. 217–19.

24 Lee 2000, pp. 133–37.

25 Crow 1996, pp. 131ff.

26 For requisite hand wringing, see Kramer 2007.

27 Feldman composed a piece for voice, viola, celeste, and percussion specifically for the Rothko Chapel in Houston. Feldman found in Rothko's color-field paintings a visual instantiation of the experience of what he called "scale." Moreover, Feldman, who was an intimate of the Eighth Street painters like Rauchenberg and Guston, felt that he imported from certain Abstract Expressionist paintings elements that had to do with the artistic expression of stasis. By extension this amounts to yet another way to look at the relation of architecture to music—they may have shared *structures*. Feldman's concern in his late works with the musical presentation of a kind of ecstatic stasis—which he also gleaned from his close relationship to Cage's music and his study of Turkish rugs—puts his music in very interesting relation to architecture. In what follows, we shall discuss music and architecture as analogs in terms that involve movement, a dynamism that Feldman

might be seen to undermine. A fine recording of Feldman's *Rothko Chapel* is available from the California EAR Unit and the University of California Chamber Chorus on New Albion 039CD (1991).

28 The best treatment of the relation of architectural Baroque to neo-classicism is still Kaufmann 1955.

29 An excellent treatment of these composers along this line is Rosen 1971.

30 More specifically, in connection with Dionysian festivals, the dance was a *choros kuklios*—a circular dance around an altar.

31 Silk & Stern 1981 contains an excellent treatment of the stagecraft and architecture of Greek drama and their relation to Nietzsche.

32 Randel 1986, p. 225.

33 It is usual in music theory to distinguish rather sharply between true development of a theme and its mere variation. A variation is a shift in emphasis, texture, or even tonality within a theme that leaves in place the thematic structure. Some musicologists hold that what romantic composers thought was thematic development is, analytically speaking, very complicated variation. The line is hard to draw. Schoenberg exploits this difficulty, arguing for a category of "developing variation" applicable to serialism. Schoenberg deploys this concept dialectically to refer to structural alteration that must be viewed musicologically from two sides at once. On the one hand, the structure undergoes variation and, therefore, presupposes identity of theme. One can only vary a theme that persists as the same theme over the variation of it. On the other hand, the structure develops because it does not merely repeat material in a new way. By pitching his own music on the knife's edge between variation and development, Schoenberg points to the collapse of those terms into one another, once traditional musical practice in terms of traditional harmony is repudiated. He believes that his own twelve-tone compositions do not require, and indeed prohibit, a strict separation of the two ideas. He seems to have also believed that Brahms was the composer who first questioned the distinction.

34 There is a third basis (or fourth—see note 27) on which it has been argued that music and architecture can be considered in terms of one another. Some architectural theorists have viewed architecture and music as stemming from a shared foundation in representing nature, the more "natural" the better. For instance, it seems that the eighteenth-century theorist Briseux found a great deal in common between his

views on natural proportion and Rameau's treatment of musical tonality. See Pérez Gomez (1983). This strand of thought about music and architecture as forms of natural representation or even mimicry is not very convincing today.

35 Chatman 1985, pp. 101–13 is an interesting treatment of these issues that also sees a connection with de Chirico.

36 A former angel is played by the actor Peter Falk, playing himself. In several parts of the film he is identified by passers-by as Columbo, a reference to Falk's role as the disheveled detective in the 1970s television series of the same name. He is present in Berlin to play the role in a film of a detective very similar in appearance to the Columbo character and dresses accordingly.

37 In fact, the film hedges a bit on the degree to which the angelic and human worlds are ontologically separate. In the famous sequence in the Berlin Staatsbibliothek an angel "picks up" a spectral pencil that corresponds to the physical article as it is used by one of the humans. This kind of twilight world between the angelic and human worlds is repeated later in the film in a scene in which one of the angels picks up a stone when visiting the dressing-trailer of his human lover-to-be, a circus trapeze artist. These superimposition effects are not unique to *Wings of Desire*, nor is their association with spirits interacting with the physical world.

38 The cinematographer for the film, Henri Alekan, had shot Jean Cocteau's *Beauty and the Beast*, often cited as the single most beautiful black-and-white film. The film is not simple black-and-white stock: there are subtle hues of silvered tan akin to a silver gelatin photographic print. Alekan used an antique silk stocking (apparently his grandmother's) as a filter for the black-and-white sequences.

39 Gregg Horowitz points out to me that the choice of smoking as expressive of human corporeal freedom has political undertones. Hitler was violently anti-smoking and post-war Germans took this—in their inimitably Kantian way—to posit an imperative to smoke (i.e., as an anti-fascist credential). Of course, there is the point of the connection between a pleasure that kills and mortality as well.

40 Commentators on the film always stress the aspiration of the angels to the human condition and its limit case—the desire to be human. Hardly anyone notes that humans have the inverse desire. They aspire to be free

of human limitations like pain, hunger, worry, death, etc. What is a trapeze artist, other than someone who is suspended between heaven and earth? More than that, she is someone who presents such a suspension for one's entertainment. I thank Leslie Callahan for pointing out the importance of the image of the trapeze artist in this context to me.

41 Deictic music is music that is portrayed as present to the characters within the film—a band playing, a radio broadcast, etc. A well-known example would be the nightclub scene in Antonioni's *Blow Up* featuring the Jeff Beck incarnation of the Yardbirds. Non-deictic music is what is generally referred to as soundtrack, although that broad term technically includes both sorts of music present in film. By "pure vocalization" I mean voices without syntax or semantics (i.e., no words, just sounds).

42 Tr. R. Fagles & ed. B. Knox (New York: Viking, 1996).

THREE   BUILDINGS, BUILDINGS, AND MORE BUILDINGS

1 Of course, one might do this if the surroundings were unappealing, run down, etc. Rationales for urban renewal have often resulted in such statements. But they are often met with competing claims to preserve the character of the given surroundings, if in a much better form. The point is that not many architects will be idealistic enough to push a project in terms of how much it will disrupt a site.

2 See Fig. 1.3, Chapter 1.

3 Weyergraf-Serra & Buskirk 1991 is an interesting blow-by-blow documentation of the *Tilted Arc* affair.

4 For a lively and insightful discussion of the vicissitudes of sanitation in eighteenth-century Paris, see Sennett 1994, pp. 263ff.

5 Koolhaas & Mau come close to this view. See Koolhaas & Mau 1998, pp. 969ff.

6 One immediate objection is that sheer variety is not necessarily good. Variation among slag-heaps is likely neither to enrich architectural experience nor to be very instructive generally. One also might think that too much variation would overwhelm human experiential capacities, especially if there is something like a native capacity to categorize or form a generally coherent experience out of experiential components. I ignore these concerns in what follows.

7 Gropius 1943.

8 Frampton 1992, pp. 181–2.

9 Wright did not invent the word, although it is difficult to say where he picked it up. Perhaps he nicked it from John Dos Passos' *U.S.A.* trilogy, where it is deployed.

10 Sennett 1990, p. 173.

11 I return to this point below.

12 Mumford 1961.

13 Mumford took his idea to the mass medium of film, writing the narration for *The City* (1939), a documentary on the inhumanity of the modern city. Contrasted with the city of the title is the bucolic rural New England village and, specifically, the town of Greenbelt, where a marriage of "clean, healthy living" and "modern convenience" is to be effected. Scored by Aaron Copeland, the film played on fairgrounds across America. See Ross 2007, pp. 288–89.

14 For a consideration of the effects in America, see Rybczynski 1995, pp. 173ff.

15 Jacobs 1972, p. 33.

16 See Duany, Plater-Zyberk, & Speck 2000, ch. 4; cf. Lynch 1960, ch. 1, especially on "legibility" and "imageability." Lynch studied at Taliesin under Wright.

17 Duany, Plater-Zyberk, & Speck 2000, pp. 48ff., 60–61.

18 Förster was the husband of Nietzsche's sister Elisabeth, who doctored parts of his unpublished notes to proto-fascist ends and published them after Nietzsche's death as *The Will to Power*. Förster was an alcoholic swindler, bankrupted the colony, and finally committed suicide in a fleabag hotel.

19 Steven Holl designed the community center in Seaside. It is apparently one of the most unloved buildings in the town.

20 Duany, Plater-Zyberk, & Speck 2000, pp. 74ff. Cf. Koolhaas & Mau 1998, pp. 960ff.

21 Pallasmaa 2005.

22 There are exceptions in modern architecture of course. Leatherbarrow 2000 argues persuasively that Richard Neutra is one. For Neutra's own views, see the essays collected in Neutra 1969, especially ch. 21.

23 Sartre also denied this in his main phenomenological work, *Being and Nothingness* (1943), but came to think that the phenomenological ontology developed in that book could be extended in ethical directions. See Sartre 1992.

Bibliography

Arnheim, Rudolf, 1977. *The Dynamics of Architectural Form*. Berkeley: University of California Press.

Bachelard, Gaston, 1969 [1957]. *The Poetics of Space*, tr. M. Jolas. Boston: Beacon.

Baxandall, Michael, 1995. *Shadows and Enlightenment*. New Haven: Yale University Press.

Benjamin, Andrew, 2000. *Architectural Philosophy*. London & New Brunswick: Athlone.

Bloomer, Kent & Moore, Charles, 1977. *Body, Memory, and Architecture*. New Haven: Yale University Press.

Caldwell, Michael, 2007. *Strange Details*. Cambridge, MA: M.I.T. Press.

Chatman, Seymour, 1985. *Antonioni, or, the Surface of the World*. Berkeley: University of California Press.

Crow, Thomas, 1996. *Modern Art in the Common Culture*. New Haven: Yale University Press.

De Botton, Alain, 2006. *The Architecture of Happiness*. New York: Pantheon.

Dodds, George & Tavernor, Robert, 2002. *Body and Building: Essays on the Changing Relation of Body and Architecture*. Cambridge, MA: M.I.T. Press.

Dreyfus, Hubert, 1991. *Being-in-the-world*. Cambridge, MA: M.I.T. Press.

Duany, Andres, Plater-Zyberk, Elizabeth, & Speck, Jeff, 2000. *Suburban Nation: The Rise of Sprawl and the Decline of the American Dream*. New York: Farrar, Straus & Giroux.

Eco, Umberto, 1986. *Art and Beauty in the Middle Ages*, tr. H. Bredin. New Haven: Yale University Press.

Frampton, Kenneth, 1992. *Modern Architecture: A Critical History*, 3rd rev. edn. London: Thames & Hudson.

—— , 1995. *Studies in Tectonic Culture: The Poetics of Construction in Nineteenth and Twentieth Century Architecture*, ed. J. Cava. Cambridge, MA: M.I.T. Press.

On Architecture

——— , 2003. *Steven Holl: Architect*. Milan: Electa.

Fried, Michael, 1967. "Art and Objecthood," *Artforum* 5 (June): 12–23.

——— , 1980. *Absorption and Theatricality: Painting and Beholder in the Age of Diderot*. Chicago: University of Chicago Press.

Gins, Madeline & Arakawa, 2002. *Architectural Body*. Tuscaloosa: University of Alabama Press.

Goodman, Nelson, 1976. *Languages of Art*, 2nd edn. Indianapolis: Hackett.

——— , 1988. "How Buildings Mean," in Goodman, Nelson & Elgin, Catherine, *Reconceptions in Philosophy and Other Arts and Sciences*, pp. 31–48. Indianapolis: Hackett.

Gropius, Walter, 1943. *Scope of Total Architecture: A New Way of Life*. New York: Harper.

——— , 1965. *The New Architecture and the Bauhaus*. Cambridge, MA: M.I.T. Press.

Gutting, Gary, 2001. *French Philosophy in the Twentieth Century*. Cambridge & New York: Cambridge University Press.

Harries, Karsten, 1998. *The Ethical Function of Architecture*. Cambridge, MA: M.I.T. Press.

Hegel, G.W.F., 1975 [1835]. *Aesthetics: Lectures on Fine Art*, tr. T.M. Knox. Oxford: Oxford University Press.

Heidegger, Martin, 1962 [1927]. *Being and Time*, tr. J. Macquarrie & E. Robinson. New York: Harper & Row.

——— , 1971. *Poetry, Language, Thought*, tr. A. Hofstadler. New York: Harper & Row.

Herder, J.G., 2006. *Selected Writings in Aesthetics*, tr. and ed. G. Moore. Princeton: Princeton University Press.

Hitchcock, Henry-Russell, 1929. *Modern Architecture: Romanticism and Reintegration*. London: Payson & Clarke.

Holl, Steven, 1989. *Anchoring*. New York: Princeton Architectural Press.

——— , 1996. *Intertwining*. New York: Princeton Architectural Press.

——— , 2000. *Parallax*. New York: Princeton Architectural Press.

Holl, Steven, Pallasmaa, Juhani, & Pérez-Gomez, Alberto (eds.), 2006. *Questions of Perception: Phenomenology of Architecture*, rev. edn. San Francisco: A+U.

Huizinga, J., 1965. *The Waning of the Middle Ages*, tr. F. Hopman. London: Penguin.

Hurley, Susan, 1998. *Consciousness in Action*. Cambridge, MA: Harvard University Press.

Husserl, Edmund, 1956–. *Gesammelte Werke*, ed. Husserliana. Dordrecht: Kluwer.

—— , 1973. *Experience and Judgment*, ed. & tr. K. Ameriks & J.S. Churchill. Evanston, IL: Northwestern University Press.

Jacobs, Jane, 1972. *The Death and Life of Great American Cities: The Failure of Town Planning.* London: Penguin.

Kant, Immanuel, 1928 [1790]. *The Critique of Judgement*, tr. J.C. Meredith. Oxford: Oxford University Press.

Kaufmann, Emil, 1955. *Architecture in the Age of Reason: Baroque and Post-Baroque in England, Italy, and France.* Cambridge, MA: Harvard University Press.

Kivy, Peter, 1984. *Sound and Semblance: Reflections on Musical Representation.* Princeton: Princeton University Press.

Koolhaas, Rem & Mau, Bruce, 1998. *S,M,L,XL*, 2nd edn. New York: Monacelli.

Kramer, Lawrence, 2007. *Why Classical Music Still Matters.* Berkeley: University of California Press.

Krauss, Rosalind, 1985. *The Originality of the Avant-Garde and Other Modernist Myths.* Cambridge, MA: M.I.T. Press.

—— , 1991. "Overcoming the Limits of Matter: on Revising Minimalism," in *American Art of the 1960s*, ed. J. Elderfield. MoMA Studies in Modern Art, No. 1, pp. 123–41. New York: MoMA/Abrams.

Kristeller, Paul Oskar, 1951–2. "The Modern System of the Arts," *Journal of the History of Ideas* 12: 496–527 & 13: 17–46.

Lawrence, A.W., 1967. *Greek Architecture*, 2nd edn. Baltimore: Penguin.

Leatherbarrow, David, 2000. *Uncommon Ground: Architecture, Technology, and Topography.* Cambridge, MA: M.I.T. Press.

Le Corbusier [Jeanneret, Charles Edouard], 1982. *Manière de penser l'urbanisme: soigner la ville malade*, rev. edn. Paris: Denoël.

—— , 1986 [1923]. *Towards a New Architecture*, tr. F. Etchelle. New York: Dover.

Lee, Pamela, 2000. *Object to be Destroyed: The Work of Gordon Matta-Clark.* Cambridge, MA: M.I.T. Press.

Lefebvre, Henri, 1991 [1974]. *The Production of Space*, tr. D. Nicholson-Smith. London: Blackwell.

Libeskind, Daniel, 2000. *The Space of Encounter.* New York: Universal.

Lynch, Kevin, 1960. *The Image of the City.* Cambridge, MA: M.I.T. Press.

Mostafavi, Mohsen & Leatherbarrow, David, 1993. *On Weathering.* Cambridge, MA: M.I.T. Press.

Mumford, Lewis, 1961. *The City in History.* New York: Harcourt Brace Jovanovich.

Neutra, Richard, 1969. *Survival through Design*, 2nd edn. Oxford: Oxford University Press.

Noë, Alva, 2006. *Action in Perception*. Cambridge, MA: M.I.T. Press.

Norberg-Schulz, Christian, 1985. *The Concept of Dwelling: On the Way to Figurative Architecture*. New York: Rizzoli.

——, 1990. *Meaning in Western Architecture*. New York: Rizzoli.

O'Shaughnessy, Brian, 1980. *The Will: A Dual Aspect Theory*, 2 vols. Cambridge: Cambridge University Press.

——, 2003. *Consciousness and the World*. Oxford: Oxford University Press.

Pallasmaa, Juhani, 2005. *The Eyes of the Skin: Architecture and the Senses*. London: Wiley & Sons.

Panofsky, Erwin, 1946. *Abbot Suger on the Abbey Church of St.-Denis and Its Art Treasures*. Princeton: Princeton University Press.

Pérez Gomez, Alberto, 1983. *Architecture and the Crisis of Modern Science*. Cambridge, MA: M.I.T. Press.

Pevsner, Nikolaus, 1981. *An Outline of European Architecture*, 7th rev. edn. New York: Penguin.

Quine, W.V.O., 1960. *Word and Object*. Cambridge, MA: M.I.T. Press.

Randel, D.M. (ed.), 1985. *The New Harvard Dictionary of Music*. Cambridge, MA: Harvard University Press.

Rasmussen, Steen Eiler, 1959. *Experiencing Architecture*. Cambridge, MA: M.I.T. Press.

Rosen, Charles, 1971. *The Classical Style: Haydn, Mozart, Beethoven*. New York: Norton.

Ross, Alex, 2007. *The Rest Is Noise: Listening to the Twentieth Century*. New York: Farrar, Straus & Giroux.

Ruskin, John, 1960 [1853]. *The Stones of Venice*, abr. edn., ed. J.G. Links. New York: Farrar, Straus & Giroux.

Ruskin, John, 1989 [1880]. *The Seven Lamps of Architecture*. New York: Dover.

Rybczynski, Witold, 1995. *City Life*. New York: Simon & Schuster.

Sartre, Jean-Paul, 1992. *Notebooks for an Ethics*, tr. D. Pellauer. Chicago: University of Chicago Press.

Schelling, F.W.J., 1989 [1859]. *Philosophy of Art*, tr. D. Stott. Minneapolis: University of Minnesota Press.

Schopenhauer, Arthur, 1969 [1819/44]. *The World as Will and Representation*, tr. E.F.J. Payne. New York: Dover.

Scruton, Roger, 1979. *The Aesthetics of Architecture*. Princeton: Princeton University Press.

Sennett, Richard, 1990. *The Design and Social Life of Cities*. New York: Knopf.

—— , 1994. *Flesh and Stone: The Body and the City in Western Civilization*. New York: Norton.

Silk, M.S. & Stern, J.P., 1981. *Nietzsche on Tragedy*. Cambridge: Cambridge University Press.

von Simson, Otto, 1956. *The Gothic Cathedral: Origins of Gothic Architecture and the Medieval Concept of Order*. New York: Pantheon.

Skinner, B.F., 1953. *Science and Human Behavior*. New York: Macmillan.

Suger, Abbé, 1867. *Oeuvres complètes*, ed. A. Lecoy de la Marche. Paris.

Tschumi, Bernard, 1996. *Architecture and Disjunction*. Cambridge, MA: M.I.T. Press.

Venturi, Robert, 1977. *Complexity and Contradiction in Architecture*. 2nd edn. New York: MoMA.

Venturi, Robert, Brown, Denise Scott, & Izenour, Steven, 1997. *Learning from Las Vegas*, rev. edn. Cambridge, MA: M.I.T. Press.

Vitruvius [Pollio], Marcus, 1960. *The Ten Books on Architecture*, tr. M.H. Morgan. New York: Dover.

Weyergraf-Serra, Clara & Buskirk, Martha, 1991. *The Destruction of Tilted Arc: Documents*. Cambridge, MA: M.I.T. Press.

Wolfe, Tom, 1981. *From Bauhaus to Our House*. New York: Farrar, Straus & Giroux.

Index